Praise for *Fight the Fear*

'Mandie's enthusiasm will be felt as you progress through this book, taking inspiration from her journey and assisting you to build your own confidence along the way. It provides a sound and practical framework to enable you to tackle any fears you may have, providing advice on how to overcome them, giving your chances of future success a massive boost.'

Mike Smith, Senior Inward Investment, Economy and Growth Officer, Chelmsford City Council

'A triumphant book – Mandie's unique ability to motivate and inspire abounds within its pages. It will make you think about your fears in a new light, and ensure you take action to overcome them.'

Nigel Risner, motivational and inspirational speaker

'Exactly what I expected from Mandie, an absolutely fantastic book full of practical tips, advice and strategies to help you kick the fears holding you back and get you well on your way to success!'

Sarah Hurley, Director, Sarah Hurley Ltd

'This book is a no frills, no jargon, easy to read guide to losing the fears that hold you back in business. A great read with practical, simple steps to help you conquer the fears that hold you back.'

Melissa Neisler Dickinson, Managing Director, The Suffolk Wedding Show

'If you are someone who wants to take control of your life and do it right now then this is the book for you. Mandie is an incredible person who has helped so many people break free from what has held them back and then helped and supported them in developing the confidence to achieve their goals. The reason this book is so good is that it tackles the number one issue that holds most people back – and that's fear.

Once people learn how to see through the illusion that fear can often be they can achieve their goals, dreams and ambitions much more easily. This is a book that is packed with tips, tools, strategies and techniques to conquer fear and live your life to the full. I would highly recommend this book to anyone that wants to supercharge their life.'

Pete Cohen, life coach, motivational speaker and bestselling author

'Mandie helped me realise my dreams, and I am eternally grateful to her triggering that special spark – not only to ignite my passion but turn it into a successful and profitable business.'

Angela Chouaib, MD and founder, www.SecretSurgery.co.uk

'Mandie's book makes such impressive sense and, even better, it is easy to read. It provides clarity in a world that is so fast paced. Whilst Mandie remains "bossy" by including exercises and homework, she allows us to gain far more through actions and working out what matters to us. Sometimes it takes a while to recognise that someone has a special ability to get us to believe in ourselves, to tie that belief to our highest ideals, and to imagine that together we can do great things. In those rare moments, when such a person comes along, we need to put aside our plans and reach for what we know is possible.'

Jo-Anne Stewart, 'New Openings' Project Manager, Premier Inn, and hub by Premier Inn

Fight the Fear

Fight the Fear

How to beat your negative mindset and win in life

MANDIE HOLGATE

Harlow, England • London • New York • Boston • San Francisco • Toronto • Sydney
Auckland • Singapore • Hong Kong • Tokyo • Seoul • Taipei • New Delhi
Cape Town • São Paulo • Mexico City • Madrid • Amsterdam • Munich • Paris • Milan

Pearson Education Limited
Edinburgh Gate
Harlow CM20 2JE
United Kingdom
Tel: +44 (0)1279 623623
Web: www.pearson.com/uk

First edition published 2017 (print and electronic)

Pearson Education is not responsible for the content of third-party internet sites.

ISBN: 978–1–292–15595–1 (print)
      978–1–292–15596–8 (PDF)
      978–1–292–15597–5 (ePub)

British Library Cataloguing-in-Publication Data
A catalogue record for the print edition is available from the British Library

Library of Congress Cataloging-in-Publication Data
A catalog record for the print edition is available from the Library of Congress

10 9 8 7 6 5 4 3 2
20 19 18 17 16

Cover design by Two Associates

Print edition typeset in 10 and ITC Giovanni Std by SPi Global
Printed by Ashford Colour Press Ltd, Gosport

NOTE THAT ANY PAGE CROSS REFERENCES REFER TO THE PRINT EDITION

To Andy, Harrison and Sophie,
because you make me
fearless – thank you.

Contents

About the author

Mandie Holgate is a business coach, author, trainer, speaker and founder of The Business Woman's Network. She was one of the UK's youngest body shop managers in the automotive industry, with a passion for people's success. Mandie has spent many years enabling people to appreciate their true potential, overcome their fears, increase their confidence and achieve their big goals to success.

Within three years of setting up her own business, Mandie had been hailed as a 'good writer' by Stephen Fry, been invited to hear the Home Secretary speak on the success of women in business and appeared on UK TV and in most of the UK national newspapers.

Despite serious illness, Mandie believes anything is possible with the right mindset, actions and support. Mandie can 'fix' people's fears of public speaking or using the phone for business in just one session. She works for the third sector, enterprise agencies, national government business growth initiatives, corporate clients and individuals. Kay Westrap has said, 'In 25 years of corporate finance, I can honestly say you are the best most inspirational speaker I have ever seen, male or female'.

Mandie's tagline is 'I'm as passionate about your success as you are', and her clients can attest that she means it.

Introduction

Not all fear leaves you sweating, fearing for your life or screaming and running for the hills. However, when it comes to success, 'fear' is a word I hear many times:

▶ 'I can't turn this down. I'm too scared of what the consequences might be.'
▶ 'I'm frightened of what they might say.'
▶ 'I couldn't let anyone find that out, that's just too scary!'
▶ 'I can't do that!'

Fear lurks behind so many elements of our lives, and to be successful you need to find ways to battle it. You must find where it hides and eradicate it.

As a child you had someone there to hold your hand and coax you forward and keep the momentum going, to guide you into action and help you find a way forward. However, as an adult it's all too easy to stagnate, to stall and allow life to slow down. You 'accept' where you find yourself and enable fear to take over.

Before I wrote this book, I hadn't really thought about how badly fear can attack success. I would have thought that most people around me are not that frightened; and yet, as I think back over the years of coaching clients and supporting people to get the results they want in their personal and professional lives, I have analysed these sessions and realised that, in actual fact, fear had a massive impact on so many people's results.

So, I reasoned, wouldn't it be great if someone would be so kind as to put that information into a no-nonsense, easy-to-read book (because, let's be honest, we are all mega busy) that would sink into your brain faster than red wine into a carpet, and enable your subconscious to pick up on these brilliant ideas to help you override those fears that are secretly sabotaging your success.

And before you put this book down and tell me you're a fearless superhero who can achieve anything, I have had many a successful entrepreneur before me who has realised in a 'light bulb' moment that they too 'hide' behind a plethora of things at the most inopportune moment. It is truly scary how fear can sneak secretly into your mentality and erode your success. So, for the sake of your success, it's worth a few moments of your time, right?

So here's the thing about reading my book. ('Wow', you think, 'we have not even started the first chapter and already she's getting bossy!') That's fine, I get that a lot, but I don't want to waste one of the most valuable commodities you will ever have – time – so let's make this time we spend together really count OK? I do tend to be straight talking!

When I work with people, be it one-to-one or in a room of hundreds, I still set homework. You need to put effort into the things that matter in life, right? So with each chapter I promise:

▶ not to use jargon;
▶ to give you *real* content;
▶ to give you *real* solutions that I know could change your success rate (and your life).

And, in return, I just ask that if I set a tiny little exercise, you actually do it. I will make the big assumption that you:

▶ are mega busy;
▶ are up against deadlines;
▶ want a social life – that you don't want to be chained to work and want to live a life that fulfils you and the ones you love.

With that in mind, it's my job to ensure the homework I set will realistically fit into a very busy life. So if you read a chapter, do yourself a favour and do the homework!

How this book works and how to read it

Each chapter is neatly packaged with examples, exercises and actions and, best of all, the kind of results you can expect to achieve so that you too can win at work. Let me explain the structure of the chapters so that you can easily utilise them. To really make this book work, you will need to take action AND do the exercises. So, to help you remember how this book works, I've created this nifty little acronym: F E A R

▶ Section 1 – F: The fear.
▶ Section 2 – E: Examples and exercises.

▶ Section 3 – A: Actions
▶ Section 4 – R: Results.

Let me explain:

Section 1: The fear

Not all fear waves its arms in the air and shouts, 'Cooooee, I'm a big evil fear and I'm wrecking your success at work!' Some fear hides in your subconscious and attacks your results without you realising, and it's hard to spot what these fears actually look like. So, unless you are lucky enough to work with a coach, you may miss that 'eureka!' or 'light bulb' moment, where clients say to me, 'I can't believe this has been impacting on my success!' And, as with so many obstacles to success, when you know it exists, it is far easier to deal with it. So the start of each chapter will explore what this fear does, how it manifests itself, how it attacks your success and what impact it can have.

Section 2: Examples and exercises

Maybe you don't have time to read the whole book; maybe you feel like you are having a tough day, or you're facing a big presentation or a new challenge that is proving scary. Examples of other people's trials are a great way to see how fears play out in our lives and can help you to understand how they could be affecting your own success. So instead of reading the whole chapter, you can dip into this section of the book and get a quick 'morsel' that will get you through the day. Then you can come back later to get the full three courses that will whip that fear out of your life for good.

The exercises in this book are the backbone of so many sessions with my clients, and they can really help you understand a natural way of thinking, working, learning and show you what you really want in life. They also showcase some of the ideas we put into action so that you can trial them for yourself. This is exciting stuff and I can't wait to share it with you!

Section 3: Action

In life it's great to talk about what you want to achieve, it's great to appreciate what you are doing wrong; however, this talk is pretty useless without action. The action section of each chapter will help you reinforce the exercises to ensure you take action. It will help you improve your success rate and keep the momentum going.

Section 4: Results

Here we will look at what results you can expect to see if you take action and, more disconcertingly, what might happen if you continue not to take action. It's a powerful motivator to know what you are agreeing to. So in the final part of each chapter we will look at the results that you could get stuck with if you don't deal with this fear.

The best bit about this book is that if you picked it up because you have a fear or public speaking, or you worry too much about what everyone else is thinking, then that's fine. You've read the intro to understand how this book works, so go for it! You need to read Chapter 1 because there is a priceless exercise in there that could change your life. You can just read the chapters you need. However, as you read you may become aware that fear has a habit of hiding. Not all fear is the same. Not all fear is a monster the size of a house, ready to frighten you every time you step outside your front door. Some fears play out in your head every day, but they've become an inner voice you are so used to hearing that you just accept them as normal. So it may be worth going back to Chapter 1 and exploring the book more if these fears are lurking as obstacles in the road to your success.

I will ask a few favours of you.

- ▶ **Do the exercises.** Even if you are reading this last thing at night, commuting to work or worn out and wishing you were elsewhere, but desperate for some solutions, my promise to you is that I've made the exercises easy to read and action because I appreciate how busy your head is and I know you need easy solutions.
- ▶ **Don't be too hard on yourself.** We are far nicer to other people than we are to ourselves. You have just gained a coach who is going to help work on yourself in a way that you may never have done before. On a deeper level, that could actually change your success rate. The 'shout at someone until they do it' approach doesn't work, so don't do it to yourself either.
- ▶ **Trust that you can change.** With the support of this book, you can change, because I'm here to support you to do it. Let's do this!

What if someone finds out who I really am?

F – The fear

Can it really be a fear of saying who you really are? So often we hide what we really want, who we really are and what we really enjoy in life for fear that other people may not approve. And why is that an obstacle to success? Because if you can't be honest about the fact that you enjoy a staycation, that you like cats, that you have children who light up your life, that you like model aircraft or enjoy knitting or you've always wanted to go on the Orient Express, how are you going to be honest and tell someone that you actually don't want to sit on the board of directors, or that actually you DO want to sit on the board of directors?

And, likewise, when you *get* the things you want in life, how are you going to *keep* them if you are constantly second guessing and looking over your shoulder thinking, 'What if someone finds out who I really am?'

If we are going to look at the real challenges to success, we have to start by looking at what you want in life. And one of the reasons why people don't achieve success that matters to them and that they can really feel, is because they crave the wrong things. They go for goals and ambitions created for them by the outside world and by other people rather than by their internal values, passions and desires.

❝ If we are going to look at the real challenges to success, we have to start by looking at what you want in life. ❞

In the office it's assumed you would want the top job. If you own your business it's assumed you want a global empire with offices around the world. Why wouldn't you want to be a millionaire? Everyone wants that, right?

If you want true success, you need to be able to confidently and succinctly say '*This* is what I want' and to not be worried about what anyone else thinks. And yet it's easier said than done, so Chapter 10 will be helpful for this too. To really power up your success, you can't fight the person you really are. You have to learn to stop hiding behind what you think everyone needs you to be, or what you think people think you should be.

When things in life don't fit comfortably with the person you really are, it works against your success. You find yourself doing things you don't want to do, working on things that you don't enjoy, towards goals that don't fulfil you. Life lacks joy, excitement and passion. The people sharing those 'Only five days until the weekend' posters on social media are probably fighting the true version of themselves. They are filling their professional days with things that do not inspire and fulfil them. They put money in the bank and that's about it.

In our world, from the moment we wake until, quite often, the moment we sleep, we're receiving information. Even the journey to work isn't safe. Everywhere is full of things that assault your senses. You can know what someone had for breakfast on the other side of the world, whether they ate papaya sitting on the beach or porridge on the back of a yacht. You can watch videos of the wildest commutes to work or people working from the most beautiful places in the world. Someone online will have it bigger and better than you: a faster car, bigger house, a bigger TV, more shoes, more hair, more money. And we are constantly manipulated as a consumer to purchase, believe and desire. Scary, right? No wonder it can become hard to find what you really want out of life. And it's sometimes hard to even appreciate you are on that treadmill, being pulled along with the flow.

"We are constantly manipulated as a consumer to purchase, believe and desire."

E – Examples and exercises

Example

On many occasions I have asked an audience, 'Who in this room wants to own a Ferrari?' What do you think the answer should be? Should it be a room full of arms shooting up? Should it be a few 'Yes pleases!' What would you expect?

In my experience only one or two hands go up. And then when I challenge those two brave souls who gingerly wave their hand near their ears I ask, 'If you really want that Ferrari, why is your hand not shooting high in the air like when you were six, when you were practically being rocket-launched out of your chair you were that desperate to tell your teacher the answer?'

You see, if you *really* want a Ferrari then it's a passion, an internal motivator that you can feel with every fibre of your body, and the minute you see the word, hear the word or see the image your body is alive with excitement and passion to know more.

Whenever I have ever used this example I have never seen that level of passion and excitement and never felt that feeling of 'Wow I'm going to explode with love at first site if I don't get to speak in the next Nano second!'

That, reader, is real passion. You need to find what your goals are in life, to work out what your internal motivators are, and find the confidence to be the real you. Find what makes you feel so alive that, as you read this sentence, you can feel your heart beating faster, a smile growing on your face and your mind wandering off as you daydream about the results. That is a passion, a goal. And all too often we hide what we really want and who we really are for the benefit of everyone else. And the results are that we only achieve what other people want.

‪"You need to find what your goals are in life,
to work out what your internal motivators are,
and find the confidence to be the real you."

On one occasion when I coached a client through one of the exercises in this chapter, it horrified them that a hobby was more important to them than their partner. It wasn't that clear cut. On working together, we discovered that the client did nothing to honour the things that mattered to them. They never did anything around the hobby that mattered to them. The internal drivers that made them feel alive were constantly ignored and turned off. By being aware of the values that mattered to them, they made small changes and it had a dramatic impact on their lives in all areas. It wasn't a 'them or us' situation. It didn't mean that they didn't love their partner. It was all about being aware of the values that make them as a person and knowing that, by not honouring what mattered to them, they were not feeling happy or 'alive' and that, in turn, this was having a detrimental impact on many aspects of their lives and their work.

As you will see throughout this book, not all fears jump on you at 3 o'clock in the morning screaming and yelling and keeping you up all night. Some are far subtler. And sometimes we don't even know they are there. In some ways I think these are the more frightening fears, because at least if you know a fear exists you can keep away from it. If you don't know a fear exists, it's very hard to avoid, isn't it?

Exercise – The values exercise

The first exercise in the book is paramount to so much of the knowledge you could learn about yourself, not just for helping you to be confident about the person you are and what you want in life (and getting it), but in so many other things too. It's powerful knowledge that could resonate through every aspect of your life.

Let's start by working out what matters to you. To do this you don't need to work out what the perfect life would look like; we need to forget about the outside world and think about you. What matters to you?

"What matters to you?"

You know I said that throughout this book there would be a few little bits of homework? Well here is one of them, and this is one exercise I use in my life every day. It has changed the lives of countless clients and it could be a moment in time that makes you think differently forever, so it could be worth grabbing a pen and paper. This is one of only a few exercises in the whole book that needs a little effort from you, but I promise it can be really interesting and thought provoking, and can seriously power up your results, so it's worth a go, right? It could be a 'light bulb' moment that changes your life. (In fact, just recently I used this exercise with a client and something that has literally had them stuck for years was cleared in one hour!)

1 Take a moment to think about and list the different things that matter to you. This is a confidential list that you never have to share with anyone on the planet. You don't have to justify your choices. If you want to put your children but not your partner then that is your choice, and no one is going to judge you for it. Choose 10 things – take a look at the list below for some examples. You don't have to choose from this list – you can write anything you like.

For example, the things that matter to me are: career, holidays, family, success, friends, money, hobbies, culture, work, leisure, sport, health, exercise, socialising, finances, writing, gardening, reading, music, etc.

Create a chart like this and add an item to each box, still in no particular order:

Family	
Holiday	
Fun	
Work	
Helping others	
Travel	
Writing	
Walking	
Socialising	
Money	

2 Then compare each item. For example, if you had to choose, could you live without family or holiday? If you could not live without family, then family would get one point and holiday gets a zero. Could you live without family or fun? If you could not live without fun, then fun would get 1 point and family zero. This is no reflection on your family. This is a no-guilt, for your eyes only, private document that will help you to see what matters to you. If you give family a zero it doesn't mean they don't matter to you, you are just finding out where in the great scheme of things they matter to you. So remember: no guilt, complete honestly, go with your gut instinct and write the truth!

Family	1
Holiday	0
Fun	
Work	
Helping others	
Travel	
Writing	
Walking	
Socialising	
Money	

3 Carry on moving down the column comparing family and fun, then family and work, then family and helping others, and so on. However, remember, you would be using your own list of 10, not this example list. Do this for each of the 10 items. You should end up with a chart that looks like this:

Family	111111111
Holiday	000011111
Fun	011111111
Work	010011110
Helping others	010111111
Travel	000000000
Culture	000001110
Walking	000001000
Socialising	000001010
Money	0000101111

4 With this information you can work out what your values are. For instance, with our example the top values for this person would be family, fun and helping others, because family gets 10 points, fun gets nine and helping others gets eight.

Although it is important to know the top 10 values that impact on your life, the top three are the ones that matter most to you. For this person work, holiday and money all get five points so they are not as important to them as their top three items. However, by being aware of them they will be able to factor in their genuine values to their life. This means that there will be times in their life when they need to be aware of these values and honour them. For instance, if they want to purchase something big, they know they are prepared to work hard to get it but that they still need a holiday!

Yes, it's scary to say 'These things matter to me', but you have to start somewhere, right? Have you noticed how some people seem to have the light turned off in them? They seem to have lost their glow? And yet others seem to shine, and look radiant and alive? Often when people do this exercise it throws up a surprise. Something that they thought was a lifelong value turns out to be lower down the list of priorities in their lives. By being aware of this, they can start living a life that fulfils them.

Again, I appreciate how startling it may be if you have just carried out this exercise and been thrown a curve ball; however, the scariest step is being prepared to actually take a look and see what really matters to you. Therefore, please take 10 minutes out of your day, this day, *today*, and do this exercise, and then let's look at the results and what they may mean for you.

❝Something that they thought was a lifelong value turns out to be lower down the list of priorities in their lives.❞

So, if you did the values exercise, how do you feel about what matters to you? Does it fit in snug as a bug with the person you are now? Do you feel confident and happy that you are living in the right home, driving the right car, going to work in the right place, with the right people, doing what feels like the perfect job that makes a difference to the right people? Do you feel like you are surrounded by people that nurture and complete you, and do you feel sustained and happy and like every day is a joy and gift? If yes, then, great, your fear really could lie in one of the more obvious fears. I wouldn't skip those chapters though. In my opinion, you will always learn more, even on those subjects you think you know about, because there is always another view, and there is always more you could learn.

If, on the other hand, the answer was 'No', what do you think is missing from your life?

A – Action

To help, you must find the inner confidence, and override the feeling that says the real you *has* to hide what matters to you. The person you really are is perfect, just perfect, and if you want real success in life, you need to know what that perfect version of you is all about. That way you can be proud and confident about what that person wants and desires in life. Then, no matter what comes into your life, you are able to ask yourself, 'Does this fit with the person I am?' It's good to get into the habit of asking yourself this question.

So, if you were to look around you right now, you might see a nice environment and all the things that are supposed to make you happy, but you may not be 'feeling it', because maybe one of your fears is the fear to be you. And it's all too common. It takes guts and confidence to say, 'This is what matters to me and this is what I want'. One of the reasons that people don't get the results that they want in their lives is because they are frightened to show the world what they really want. And when you get the things you want in life, just knowing it's what matters to you will help build your confidence and help you maintain and keep them too. You may need the support and help from some of the other chapters; however, by being strong and confident in the knowledge that 'this is me', you will be able to stand proud.

> **“If you want real success, you need to be prepared to say: 'This is me; this is what matters to me'.”**

If you want real success, you need to be prepared to say: 'This is me; this is what matters to me'. In the results section of this chapter you will see that by creating focused goals that really resonate with your values, you are more able to achieve them. You can stay focused on what you want and ignore the fear. Answer these questions and create some of your own. The more fun and extreme the better! And you will see as you read this book that each chapter adds more skills, strategies and exercises to really help you power up your success.

- Do you want to own a global empire?
- Do you want to sit on the board of directors?
- Do you want to sit on the parent–teacher associations?
- Do you want to sing in your local choir?
- Do you want to work in your local store?
- Do you want to be a best-selling author?
- Do you want to own your own jet?
- Do you want to run your own successful business?
- Do you want to set up your own charity?
- Do you want to sing at a football stadium?

No one has the right to tell you who you are except you. And yet, unless you define yourself this world has a habit of doing it for you. Take a moment to think about the questions you would like the answers to.

 # R – Result

When you feel confident and internally empowered about the person you are and what matters to you in life, you will be able to live in a way that makes you feel good. You will smile more too. Do you remember I started this chapter by asking 'Who wants a Ferrari?'

"When you feel confident and internally empowered about the person you are and what matters to you in life, you will be able to live in a way that makes you feel good."

What do *you* want? What ideas did the action section of this chapter create for you? So often we glaze over and go on autopilot when we hear this question. When I'm running a master class or training session and this question gets asked, I hear things like:

- I want to travel the world.
- I want to be mortgage-free.
- I want a global empire.
- I want a sports car.
- I want to make lots of money.

But when I challenge people on their answers they rarely have any details for me.

One business woman told me she wanted to make more money. So I asked her, how much more was more?

'Well you know, lots,' she said.

'How much is lots?' I asked.

You could see she was really thinking about this. The rest of the delegates were all looking at her and for the first few seconds they were wondering what she was thinking, and then I realised they had flipped their thinking to start reassessing their own goals and were digging deeper into what they really wanted. As this lady thought I could see she was struggling. So I asked:

'What do you want the money for?'

'Well I like holidays, and I've not had one for five years.'

'Okay, so where do you want to go?'

This lady went on to tell me about how she would love to go on a cruise.

'Indoor cabin or outdoors?'

'Outdoors!' she said with passion (We were getting somewhere!)

'Suite or just a nice balcony?'

'We don't need a suite; we won't be spending that much time in the room.' (Now we were really getting somewhere!)

'Is that the only holiday?' I asked

'Oh no, I'd love to take the whole family away to Portugal for a holiday.'

'Two weeks or one?' I asked.

'Only one, I don't like them that much!'

In this way, the woman was able to build a picture of how much money she wanted to earn, what she wanted to do with it and to really build up some real passion for it. Now, if she hadn't taken the time to work out what she personally wanted, she could so easily have tried to create a goal that was not harmonious to her. If she had listened to the outside world, the world of *X Factor* and Facebook, she could have created a goal that said she needed private jets and a villa in the South of France for six weeks. That wouldn't have been a goal that floated her boat. And it wouldn't have been achievable.

And I'm also pleased to say that the holidaying entrepreneur's Facebook page has been plastered with holiday snaps for the whole year!

As we've seen with our holidaying entrepreneur, you need to have clearly defined goals to get somewhere in life. And your values impact on what those goals look like. They are the backbone to your success.

"You need to have clearly defined goals to get somewhere in life."

I've also seen the impact it can have on a person's success when they *don't* stand proud about the person they are. I remember the business owner who was damaging their health, their family life and their business because they wouldn't tell the professional world that they were a parent. As if children were a crime. What message would that send to their children as they grew up? What kind of role model is that?

As we worked together, they were able to see that it was ridiculous to keep up this fakery. Okay, so there was a real risk that they could lose business, because people had grown accustomed to being able to communicate with this business owner 24/7; however, as this business owner found out, it was their 'choice' to stay 'stuck' with these customers or to move forward and 'find' customers that would respect them. It is scary to do this, and it is a sensible fear; however, with the right support and the right actions this person was able to think in a new way. They reframed their beliefs so that they could honour their core values and create goals that would make for a happy personal and professional life.

I speak from experience here: I have auto immune diseases. Now, I don't share this for you to say 'aw, poor you'. I share this because when I came back to work in 2013 after a year and a half off lying around in a dark room saying 'ouch', I had to think to myself, 'Do I risk losing out on work by being honest with people and telling them that I can only work part time, or do I lie about my capabilities?' Being a coach I knew what people were not saying as well as what they were saying. I saw it as a real risk that people in business would consider me weak if I admitted these illnesses (and in my experience, some do!). However, I appreciated I was at risk of letting it become a fear.

I wanted to test the limits of being who I really am. Was that scary? Of course. I'm not a robot. But we all have to push ourselves. As a coach, I feel that it's important that I regularly remember the real fear that my clients so often feel. I have learnt many ways over the years to remove so much fear from my life and it is only by pushing ourselves that we can constantly grow and get better results from ourselves and our lives.

Since becoming poorly, the long-haul flight holidays have been less appealing and European caravanning makes me happier. In the middle of an Internationally Celebrated Global Entrepreneur Week I told everyone I love caravanning and that I was a sick business owner. Afterwards I had the same number of people coming up and wanting to talk to me as in previous years: the same number of enquiries, bookings and opportunities and the same level of high reviews from my audience. Yes, it was scary being the real me, but being myself really was the only option. If I want to move through life feeling genuinely happy with my results and my life, it's the only option. Success will be easier to achieve if you are not putting on a pretend façade that needs to be constantly maintained. Think how much energy you could be putting into winning at work and your success if you dealt with the fear and found the strength to be true to who you are.

Would or could you have done the same?

There have been many studies that show that people don't stand up for others in a crowded environment because of the group mentality that overrides our own opinions and values. Nobody wants to stand out and speak up. If you are able to find what your values are, to be confident about them and create goals around them, then you will know that your actions are true and are taking you towards the results you want. You could still find yourself in scary situations. However, you will have the confidence to go through them because the results that you expect will far outweigh the fear. Now how fun does that sound?

Find the strength and inner confidence. Remain true to yourself so that wherever you are, and whoever you are with, you are able to get the results you want in life.

I don't want to be frivolous or glib here. I won't mind admitting in the run up to that event, I questioned if I was committing professional suicide by admitting a love of caravans and a need for rest and medication. I asked my husband on a number of occasions if he would listen to my keynote. I asked my teenage children to endure my keynote. (To teenagers, I can assure you, it's an endurance test to listen to an hour of your mother talking!) I needed to get the opinions of people who would be critical and yet honest about my work. People who knew my target audience and who wouldn't just say, 'That's nice dear', and this was something I knew I could get from my close family.

My children and I have a code. When they show me a piece of work, I will ask them 'are you wanting the a) polite reply or the b) realistic one?'

And the great thing about teenagers is they don't have an 'a' mode. Their setting is permanently on the 'b' setting. So if I was pushing my luck with my comments, I knew my kids would let me know!

And, taking into account the current trend at the time for racing caravans on the back of 'reasonably priced cars' on the UK's top TV car magazine show, I really was leaving myself open for embarrassment. Was I really going to walk into a room full of my target audience for business and do this?

"If you want to achieve your big goals and dreams you need to be able to fly in the opposite direction to a roomful of other people."

If you want to achieve your big goals and dreams you need to be able to fly in the opposite direction to a roomful of other people. In the UK we have seen a massive growth in self-employment. For women in particular, according to research by Julia Dean OBE, since 2009 women have accounted for over half of the overall growth in self-employment. And yet this is a risky path to take. It is fraught with fear and risk. By choosing self-employment, women are missing out on the chance to sit on the board of directors, to rise to the top of a FTSE company, to make CEO. Why? Are women feeling it's beyond their reach to achieve these things and choosing the easy option? Do women need training to get to the top? Or are more and more people redefining what success, goals and ambitions look like?

The increase of men taking advantage of fairer rights to paternity leave hasn't happened, despite a country poised ready for panic about the lack of skilled staff. Why? Is this another sign that people fear speaking up for the things that matter to them in life? What does that do for success? Happy people make happy staff, which is something we hear more and more. Productivity is not much improved on 1960s standards, and yet we are busier than ever, so something *has* to change. Are you ready to be a part of that? To do this you will sometimes have to tell a room full of people what your 'caravan' is. Scary? Absolutely. Worth doing? Absolutely!

"Happy people make happy staff."

You will need to gauge people's opinions. You may still experience fear to begin with. However, positive action will result in more positive reaction. It is only inertia and inaction that will allow that fear to grow and fester. Know your values, know your passions and your reasons for them.

And yet, fear could still be a deciding factor that stops you from taking action to enable the true you to walk away with the results you want. To ensure you still take the necessary action you need to look at your reasons

13

for this. If you don't honour your values, what would you be agreeing to? Ask yourself these very important questions:

▶ 'If I do not work out who I really am and if I am not prepared to stand up and be that person, then what am I agreeing to?'

▶ 'If I don't honour the person that I really am, and my values, then what am I agreeing to?'

Think back to the values exercise and the values that matter to you. What are you agreeing to live without? What are you agreeing to sacrifice? Ask yourself:

▶ 'If you continue to live in a style that does not honour your values, what impact does it have on your life?'

▶ 'What impact does it have on those that you love?'

Yes, it is scary to be the person that you want to be; however, is it not more frightening to hide the person you are meant to be? Do you remember the passion I said you needed to find what you really want? Remember the person that really wants a Ferrari? That is how you need to feel about this, as if your very being *needs* to know the answers to the questions on this page. And to be honest with you, it will be hard to achieve the big ambitions of your life if you don't, which basically means you are trapped in this chapter!

The fact is, I am speaking to you as I speak to my clients – with absolute love and a belief that you *can* get the results that you want. However, it does have to come from action, and not all action means working a 16-hour day, juicing and climbing mountains. One of the most powerful things you will ever do is to understand that you are free to choose to think what you think.

You can allow fear to be in charge. Or you can break down each fear. See how it works, see where it is in your life. Use this book to dismantle it and get what you want. So if you did take action in Chapter 1, shall we move on and set some seriously awesome goals?

Now I bet that scares the pants off you! Don't worry, we are in this together aren't we?

2

I'm scared of setting goals

F – Fear

Setting goals is not something to be done when hungover just because the date changed to the 1st of January. And this is something that has infuriated me since I was young: just after the big man has come down the chimney (that's Father Christmas, Santa, Saint Nick, etc.), there is still a house full of sweets and goodies, a ton of toys to play, it's the worst weather of the year and all you want to do is hibernate. But, according to the TV, we should be setting goals to lose weight and get fit and walk into work with the burning ambition to have the top job by Easter.

> **"Setting goals is not something to be done when hungover just because the date changed to the 1st of January."**

The other culprits for forcing goals on us that set us on a wrong footing from a young age are teachers. Sorry teachers, but you do. Teachers looked down their noses in disappointment when I said I wasn't going to university. That was their goal for me. But it was so out of sync with the person that I really was. They were completely unaware that I was so shy I wouldn't have been able to ask someone where the nearest toilet was, let alone find any of my lectures.

Don't assume a gobby teen is confident, because I most certainly wasn't. Goals are set in our lives in the weirdest way: when it's dark and cold and the house is full of tasty food, or by teachers who have never experienced anything other than education! It concerns me that in the 21st century we still don't teach about achieving goals, or about motivation and confidence building in schools.

Even now my children come home and tell me how they are doing according to grades on a piece of paper. Thankfully they live in a house where they are encouraged to think about what they want to feel, where they want to be and what do they want to be doing, rather than being asked 'What university do you want to go to?' and 'How much money do you want to earn?' (Remember money may be a core value for you; however, it's not for me or my family members. We are far more likely to achieve true success if we work according to what really floats our boat.) Thus, when you know what values excite you, how will you bring them to life? The answer is: goals.

The problem can be that people sometimes create goals that are so scary they're the equivalent of saying 'Today I'm going to walk naked down the motorway', or 'Today I will be walking two very hungry crocodiles that have not been fed for two weeks', or 'I will paint myself in my corporate colours with a sign on my head saying I'm the most successful business owner in the world with my contact details strapped on my head in a big glittery and feathered head piece, and that will get me world recognition!'

Well, quite. It *is* scary. Yes, it will get you noticed. But is it the best goal you could have set? And is it really likely you are going to go ahead with it? Have you really thought it through?

But for all my silliness, this is what so many people's goals really look like: they are poorly planned, ill advised, unachievable, unrealistic and so massively *huge*. Your brain struggles to compute it, literally!

On the other hand, other people wander along hoping that success will somehow tap them on the shoulder and say 'Hi, I understand you were looking for me?'

I can appreciate why many people shy away from setting goals altogether, or set goals that are so ambiguous that it would be sheer luck if they got there. Because somewhere in their past there could be a memory of an aunt failing at her diet by the 16th of January. Or feeling useless at school because Katie was always cleverer. (That is one I've heard so many times! So and so was so much brighter than me at school!) So what? Big deal! Why should that define your goals of success? Why should John at high school's ability to run for longer than you mean you will always believe you are less competent in the boardroom or at the meeting table?

These may seem like daft analogies; however, in my experience when you dig down with a client and explore their beliefs, you will discover that the reason they walk into a new situation or opportunity thinking 'Oh no I'm dreading this!' is because of a deep-rooted belief that says 'Yep, you have never been that good at that, have you?'

❝So ask yourself: 'What kind of goals do I set?'
Do you set goals that are too easily achieved?
Or do you set goals that are too unrealistic?❞

So ask yourself: 'What kind of goals do I set?' Do you set goals that are too easily achieved – almost so easy they're as unimpressive as telling your boss you brushed your teeth this morning? Or do you set goals that are too unrealistic – so huge you feel like giving up before you even get started? Most people would not plan their dream trip around the world and think 'Right, all I need is a pair of trainers, let's do this,' would they? So what

17

makes a goal, big AND achievable? What makes a goal scary AND achievable? What makes a goal *work*?

You don't just run around hoping for the best, shouting instructions and hoping someone heard you and will do some of what they might have heard. If you do, you are far more likely to end up feeling demotivated and stuck. People that set the wrong goals or fear setting any goals end up procrastinating and invariably don't get the results at work that they want. I see this fear manifest itself with so many professional people as negative feelings, results and actions. And all because they fear setting goals.

E – Examples and exercises

Let's shake up your attitude to goals. You may be reading this thinking, 'I already set goals!' Yes, you may do. However, are they the *right* goals? Do they make you feel a little bit like the first time you got on a bike?

Take the business owner who told me they wanted to bill more hours, but when pushed on how *many* more hours they had no idea. And when I pushed further, they had no idea how many hours the company could cope with or what their maximum capacity was! And when I pushed even further, they didn't have a clue what they wanted the company to look like in three years' time. How can you work towards a goal if you don't know what it is? Surely it's madness when attempting to win at work to set random goals with no definition, and use hope and ambiguousness and pray to the random gods of luck?

Goals should make you feel like you wish there was a hand to steady the seat for you, because it can feel really scary and that road can look really hard. Do your goals push you? Do you feel fear? If a goal doesn't make you feel a little like you are standing a little too close to the edge of a tall mountain, with a little too much breeze in your hair, then it's not the right goal.

A goal should make you say 'woo hoo!' and 'uh oh' at the same time. A goal should be scary. It should make you feel a little bit like you need to hold on to something. You should feel like you desperately want to tell someone but you are a bit scared, because if you tell someone about it, well then you have to go and do something about it, right? That means it's a good goal.

> **"A goal should you make you say 'woo hoo!'
> and 'uh oh' all at the same time."**

But it's so much more than that. And we need to help you create goals that have the right level of fear, that are right for you and only you. These three exercises will help you define your goals and give you the confidence to override the fears that stop you going for it.

Exercise 1 – Power goals

So let's start at the beginning. What do you want? What do you really want?

I want you to create a sentence that sums up what you want. For me, I imagine that I can see the words to my goal written on my forehead. Why? Because every time I wash my hands there's a mirror and in every mirror I visualise those words. When I get ready in the morning, I can see those words. When I'm driving the car, I can see the words. When I walk past a window, I can see the words. Even if I don't notice my reflection, I'm sure my subconscious spots the visualisation and keeps working on my goal, because I've a habit of hitting targets pretty quick! It's obviously not a long sentence. It's a short concise sentence that my brain knows and adores. It's so powerful I feel like I own the goal and the contents of it already!

What would be in your sentence? You need to phrase your sentence in the positive. Here are some rules to follow:

Do not include these words	Do include these words	Do add
Don't	Aim	Dates
Won't	Will	Figures
Hope	Going	Addresses
Should	Have	Times
Like	Achieve	Locations
Want	Ask for	Facts
Need	Speak	Names
Try	Concise	Amounts

Your sentence could look like this:

'I will have 10 new clients by the 16th of next month that will give me an additional income of x.'

A poor unresponsive goal could look like this:

'I will try and get some more clients in the next few months.'

Another bad example for you is:

'I won't let people take advantage of me at work anymore.'

A powerful goal could be:

'People respect me at work and appreciate me and my own goals and ambitions'.

Exercise 2 – The power of words

I don't see my working week as work. I see my working week as my time to be with people who want more out of life, and I get the joy of helping them achieve that. It's not work. I adore it. Work is a word that I associate with things that are hard. Scrubbing the barnacles off of my Dad's boat as a kid, now that was work! I used to go home with bleeding knuckles! As much fun as it was to be by the sea, the bleeding knuckles were not. So I chose to get rid of the word 'work', and I don't 'work'. In fact, when I'm gardening that too is not work, that is fun.

You see how for me there is very little work in my life? Why am I telling you this? Because I choose my words (even in my head) very carefully. I want to achieve. And I know that with what I share here with you in this book I get to achieve my goals, and I want you to get the same results. And if I use words that have negative connotations, even in my head, I risk damaging my chances of success. For me the word 'work' is a negative word. And any undesirable words that are allowed in my head can risk stopping me from taking action and can cause procrastination.

It's not just about choosing the right goals. It's not just thinking about every aspect of the goal. It's also about choosing the right words to describe your goals. The words are very, very important. The way you talk to yourself will power up your goals. For example, if you are someone that loves being outside and hates hard work and being stuck indoors, and you know that to achieve your heart's desire is going to take a lot of commitment and dedication, then use those words.

"It's not just about choosing the right goals. It's not just thinking about every aspect of the goal. It's also about choosing the right words to describe your goals."

Don't use words like 'it's going to take a ton of hard work and hours in the office'. Let's think this through. You are an outdoorsy person, who has thought big on a goal. And you know the goal is going to need things from you that take you outside of your comfort zone and stick you indoors in an office. (In Chapter 7 we will look at a massive fear for so many people and how to overcome that fear you need to get so far out of your comfort zone that you can't see it any more. Even if that fear is not one you face, the skills that we look at in that chapter will help in all aspects of your life, especially when we are looking at achieving your goals.) However, what do you do to your success if you use words that work in a very contradictory style to your natural way of thinking and your very beliefs?

Words can easily drag us down. Our minds can be easily entrenched into thinking something is too hard to achieve just by the way we choose to talk to ourselves. You can, in effect, convince yourself it is too hard. Scary right? You can literally talk yourself out of getting started on a goal, just by the way you are talking about a goal in your head! So power up your chances of success with the words you use. What words are you going to choose to use on yourself?

Exercise 3 – Break it down

When you know what you want, you need to break down every last detail of that goal. Therefore, as you plan your goals, you dismantle them. Remember to choose your words wisely. What words do you like? It sounds a bit like you are back at school and any minute now I'm going to ask you to talk about imagery, but seriously, are you a person that loves city life, the buzz and the commotion, or do you wish for peace and quiet and the sound of bird song? Think back to your values: what are your core three, what are the other seven, and how could they impact on your goal success?

We need to break your goal down into manageable pieces. If you had said to Richard Branson at 16 years of age. 'Here you go mate, here's a global empire', I wouldn't mind betting he would have struggled or at least scratched his head and thought 'Right, what do I do now?' Every great success needs to be broken down into manageable pieces. And you start in a way that works for you. And that means breaking it down, using your natural style.

There is a saying I use a lot: 'How do you eat a mountain of cheese? One bite at a time!' So look at the big picture, the big dream, the big goal. And start chipping bits a way at it. You can do this by actually writing each piece down on a notelet or creating an Excel spreadsheet. The choice is yours. Just go with your natural style of working. How would you tackle a task that you are good at?

"How do you eat a mountain of cheese?
One bite at a time!'"

Now you need to ask lots of questions. Here are a good few to get you started.

► Who is there with you?
► What does your goal look like?
► How many hours a week do you work?
► Do you work?
► Do you see it as work?
► Do you travel?
► Do you work alone?
► What needs to happen?
► Do you have all of the skills you need?
► What jobs do you hate doing? What will you probably learn to do first or outsource?
► Who can you rely on to support you to achieve this?
► Who can you rely on to give you honest feedback?
► Who will keep you on track?
► How will you know you are making progress?
► How will you overcome failure?
► How will you finance this?
► How will you stop your passion for X from getting in the way of you achieving this?
► What are you not good at?
► What beliefs do you hold about yourself that are risks to your success?
► What time scale do you need to set for the goal?
► Are you realistic in this goal?

What questions could you ask yourself? (Remember I don't know what your goal is, so considering you *do* know what your goal is, think about any additional questions you need to ask of yourself to be able to chip your big goal into manageable pieces.) I've sneaked into that list some questions

I think you need to answer to really help you succeed in your goals at work. I want to constantly recap with you:

► You need to know the person you really are.

► You need to know what you really want (and not what someone else's version of success is).

► You need to set clearly defined goals.

► You need to break goals down into manageable pieces.

For a goal to work you need to break it down. From going for a promotion to getting your products in every store in the world, whatever your burning ambitions are, whatever your goals are, you need to break them down.

A – Action

Big goals should be massive goals that make you smile from ear to ear. They should make you smile so much that you sleep the sleep of kids with a new shiny bike at the end of their beds, because you begged your parents to let you put it there, because it's such a cool present and you can't bear to be parted from it.

We started in Chapter 1 by understanding what you believed in, what mattered to you most. Now ask, what do you want? I asked you in Chapter 1 about the Ferrari. Now, if that makes you grin from ear to ear, what are you going to do to get it? If it's not a Ferrari, then what is it that you want?

Bring your goal into focus with the exercises above. And make them so clear in your mind that you can feel them. They should light up your mind as if you've already achieved them. What emotions would you be feeling if you did? Using the exercises from this chapter, what actions are you going to take?

The fear of setting goals will haunt your success at work forever unless you take action *today.* Not next week, or after this piece of work is done, or after you've finished working with this client. Today, *right now.* And remember it doesn't need to start with a grand gesture. Think back to the goal of walking naked down the motorway, with two very hungry crocodiles that have not been fed for two weeks in your corporate colours with a sign on your head to get your company known? It's extreme and it wouldn't work. There are easier and far more effective ways to achieve. So where will you choose to start?

Goals are as unique as you are. So ultimately you need to focus on just you. If your goal is going to require you to take yourself out of your comfort zone, your words will need to be powered up and to do that you will need to start by being nice to yourself. If you wouldn't say it to your best mate or your mum, then don't say it to yourself.

> **"If you wouldn't say it to your best mate or your mum, then don't say it to yourself."**

Seriously, by the end of this chapter when you've set THE goal, to get THE results you want, you need to be walking out of the door, every day saying the right things in your head. We will look at this in more detail in Chapter 4. You need to ask yourself challenging questions that ensure you have set yourself up for success. The fact is that if you believe in yourself and you hold firm to that belief, that no matter what happens, even if it all goes wrong, you will find a way forward, and you will pick yourself up. Maybe you will even have a chuckle and a nod of your head at the obstacle in your way, and then move forward. Then you will not be scared to set goals. Goals are supposed to be scary, and they are supposed to make you step back in awe for just a moment. You should think to yourself: wow, this is what I want.

R – Result

The fear of not setting goals is one that can manifest in so many ways. And ironically, with all our passion for motivational quotes and empowering posters adorning our office walls and our social media streams, it's hard to believe it's a real fear at all. However, so many professional people set goals in the wrong way. People looking to win at work can set goals that are so unachievable they cause their success rate to take a nose dive and their finances to take a dip as they invest in more personal and professional development courses and books but still use the same, wrong, methodology. If you change the method you use and access your natural style, you could drastically change your results.

> **"So many professional people set goals in the wrong way."**

Like the business owner that said they wanted to increase their agency's billable hours, but when I challenged them and asked by how much they said 'Lots!' When we delved deeper and to work out how much, it became clear that they didn't know. Thus we worked out what the company could viably look after with their current work force and what they would ideally look after in three years' time and in five years' time. (They currently saw billable hours between 40 and 120 a week.) From this we were able to create a new billable hours goal for the end of the month and for six months' time. (The homework was to figure out what one year's and three years' billable hours would look like!) Within four days they had hit their one-month goal of 500 hours. And within three weeks they had hit their target of 1,200 hours! Now that is creating a clear goal, breaking down the actions, working to your natural style and taking the right actions, and it was a joy to get a message saying they'd smashed their targets so fast.

Not all goals are big like that. Sometimes a goal is far more subtle, but just as powerful. Your goal could be to become more confident in the work place and stand up for what you believe in. For instance, I had a client who was rather shy and had great ideas, but didn't have the confidence to say what they were thinking because they were new to the company. However, their boss had made it clear they valued their opinion and wanted to see them achieve, because they saw real potential in them. The goal was set to help this person to be more vocal, confident and assertive. And the goal was achieved.

"Only you need ever know what you aim to achieve."

The joy of this process is that no one need ever know what you are doing. It is your private road to success. There is the possibility that you may wish to or need to share aspects of it with others; however, the nuts and bolts, the dismantled intricacies of your goal, are yours and yours alone. And only you need ever know what you aim to achieve. Goals are very individual, private and personal. And by honouring what matters to you and creating personal goals, you are far more likely to reach them. And then you can smile confidently and you get on with it. And that leads us nicely into Chapter 3.

CHAPTER

3

I don't believe I can succeed

F – Fear

People who want success just go for it, right? People who want success don't give up, right? The fact is, people who want success do a lot of things. And people who want success *do* get a certain way to achieving that. However, how is it possible that two people with the same experiences, the same skills, the same education, and the same opportunities can end up with different levels of success?

My dad was once labelled a fool because every summer he literally locked up his garage to take his family on holiday for six weeks. 'You are crazy!' they said. 'No one will do business with you', they said. In fact, when my father said he was going to build a big garage on a piece of wasteland, one man gave my father a £10 note and said, 'This time next year you will be worth less than that'. My father was not.

> **"How is it possible that two people with the same experiences, the same skills, the same education, and the same opportunities can end up with different levels of success?"**

How is it possible that someone whose strong values meant that nothing would come before his family time could still create a very successful business? Some would say that my father (according to today's labels) faced adversity to achieve. And yet he did win. How?

I have many stories like this. I've played a part in a good few. And I don't think the people that achieved had exceptional skills. Yes they worked hard, and yes they took the right actions and they did the things in this book. However, above all else they never faced the fear in this chapter. Or, if they did, they squashed it flat, folded it up into a little square and kicked it in the bin! It is a fear that hides in many people's subconscious, one that you are now going to challenge. You need to ask: 'Does it lie in the mind?'

I think there is far too much talking in today's society, on social media, in the traditional media, among colleagues. Talk, as they say, is indeed cheap. Talk does not get results. And yet talk can be truly damaging to your success.

Let me expand on this. Years ago we only knew another person's level of success when we saw them at work or bumped into them out and about.

'Is that so and so driving a brand new X? Wow! They must be doing alright.'

'X looks well; I see they aren't wearing fake Jimmy Choos!'

And now, we have Facebook pages of people's food. Nothing is private: everything is shared. Personally I kind of like it, but then I'm comfortable and happy with the person I am and the life I lead. However, it's all too easy to get sucked in and assume that, according to the world that you access online, everyone is driving sports cars, working every third Thursday on a beach, has perfect bodies, and is eating either enough calories for a small school or enough vitamins for a surf school, surrounded by puppies and kittens and perfect children, perfect partners and perfect homes and with perfect happy lives. Disney princesses couldn't make it more perfect.

According to some people's versions of online life there is not one bad hair day, one stroppy teenager, one cold shower or one rant at a red traffic light: everything is perfect. My inbox is plagued with people telling me they can make me happier, thinner, sell more, achieve more, be more. Everyone makes the assumption that I must hate my life. Depressing, right? Talk *is* cheap and in this chapter we are going to work on how talk is allowed to impact on your ability to succeed.

When working with clients, so often they are able to list a million failures, but when I ask them to tell me about their successes the list is not so long. That is why in Chapter 1 we looked at why you are awesome, so you had the facts to rely on when things were less than perfect. Failure is a necessary component of success.

❝Failure is a necessary component of success.❞

But so often, as someone nears the true success that they really aspire to and really crave, the failures show up and they walk away. It is when the failure feels really scary that you have got to keep going.

You may have heard Winston Churchill's legendary quote 'Never, ever, ever give up', and although it's true, I feel his sentiment has been diluted with the ocean of motivational posters and quotes plastered across our social media that have turned it into white noise. Thus, when someone is actually so very close to what they really desire they can often allow the fear to take them away from their goals.

On many occasion I've seen a business decide to re-brand, or a business owner 'go and get a real job', or someone back down from what they believe in because of this fear. And it is the fear that says 'I won't succeed'.

"What gives you the right to go through life assuming you will fail?"

What gives you the right to go through life assuming you will fail? Imagine if you got up every day and assumed you were unlikely to make it to work in the car. Or that it was statistically unlikely you would survive making a cup of coffee. What impact could that have on your mindset if you constantly assumed that death was about to happen at any moment in every day? More than anything wouldn't it be

- exhausting?
- demotivating?
- defective?

Would you want to bother getting up in the morning, since statically there was a good chance that just getting out of bed could cause death? This is similar to something that many people do with their mindset. They tell themselves that they cannot succeed, whether consciously or subconsciously. A fear lurks in your mind that says 'You will not succeed at what you wish to achieve'. In this chapter we want to look at how to deal with that fear.

How can you override that fear? How can you stop the natural instinct that kicks in as you near your ultimate goals so that, instead of changing direction, you actually keep going? When I'm working with a client the conversation can actually make a client look like a bunny trapped in the headlights of an oncoming car. They know danger is coming and yet they can't do anything; they are stuck waiting for something bad to happen, because the assumption is that something bad *is* going to happen.

Exercise 1 – Failing

Because we are bombarded by talk, by words and by everyone's input on what life looks like, we assume that that *is* life. That life is perfect and easy, that the sun always shines, so that you feel that's the only thing anyone's thinking about. There's never a 'dead battery on your laptop' kind of a day and you are the only one that bad things happen to. Think about it for a minute – why does this matter?

Well this is an unrealistic picture that is constantly put in front of your eyes, and it is damaging to your ability to achieve. Because you are constantly presented with this image of perfection you are not able to accept that true success needs failure. You see, bad stuff does happen. And bad days are part and parcel of a happy, successful winning life. And if you want real success at work, you need to accept you will have days where you want to give up. The first thing you need to do is accept that those days do happen. Not every day is a Hollywood movie kind of a day, where the hero falls in love, overcomes the baddies and gets the dream job. The bumper sticker was true: 'Sh*t happens'.

> **"Not every day is a Hollywood movie kind of day where the hero falls in love, overcomes the baddies and gets the dream job. "**

It's time to accept that bad stuff happening is good for success. There is a good chance you've heard that failure is good for success, right? Have you considered your success-to-failure ratio? How often do you succeed? How often do you fail? Do you accept and understand the need for both?

Exercise 2 – The negative spiral

When you feel like your belief in your ability to achieve is slipping away, play this game. It will enable you to step back from what is happening without taking responsibility for what is going on. We can so often feel dragged down by our problems and our worries and that can make a fear bigger and more scarier. And when fear is enabled it is empowered; when a fear is empowered it is stronger, and you can guess what *that* will do for your chances of success and winning at work.

Let's work through a negative spiral (see figure below). Think about an example of a time when you felt less capable of success. *Really* think about what it felt like. Think about a time when you felt that you were slipping from feeling positive and capable of getting results into a negative fog that made you feel that every action was pointless and moved you closer to more failure. What's the point, right? Yes *that* feeling. Let's recreate that. Think it all through. The actions, the feelings, the process.

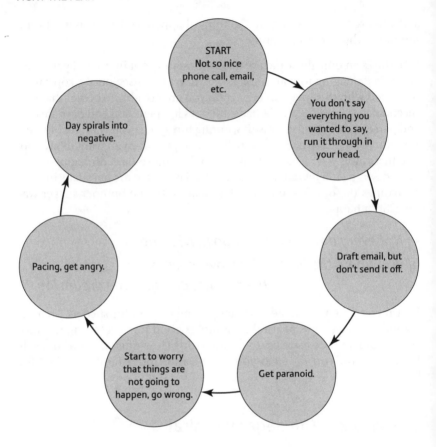

Here is an example for you:

1 You meet someone and you get talking and they like what you have to say. They ask you to send them an email outlining your ideas in more detail.

2 You don't hear from them so you make the assumption that they are not interested. (You will love Chapter 8 for this one).

3 You start to think you were a fool for ever thinking they were interested.

4 You question what you think you are doing.

5 You second guess your actions, your goals, your aspirations, your work ethic. What else?

6 You make silly mistakes at work.

7 You berate yourself.

8 You have a bad day.

9 You get home and feel miserable.

10 You can't be bothered to cook or eat right; you pour the wine and eat chocolate.

11 You sleep poorly, dream badly, worry lots and think you are a failure.

12 You wake feeling miserable and tired.

And all because you didn't get a reply to an email!

Negative spirals are easily played out, and what is scary is, as dramatic as this one is, mini versions are played out every day. If you don't recognise them and deal with them effectively, then they will grow and escalate until you can create a fear so big you literally will stop yourself from taking any action. You can believe you are incapable of your big ambitions and dreams of success. Work, life, travel, whatever you dream of. You can stop it, with a thought. Scary, right?

Now that IS a fear. The good news is that the negative spiral can be fixed in two ways.

Exercise 2 – Fix 1: The negative spiral

First, be aware of the negative spiral and spot where it starts to unravel. The first step to fixing a problem is being aware a problem exists. So find where your negativity takes root. If you are not sure, write the process out. Start at the end:

▶ What is the end result?

▶ How are you feeling now?

▶ What is the end action you take that you are not happy with?

▶ What led up to this?

"In every negative spiral I've ever worked on, the negative results started with a negative thought, not a negative action."

Work backwards from that and ask yourself questions to find out what led to that moment in time. When you find where the negativity began you can make a choice: a choice to think a different thought. In every negative spiral I've ever worked on, the negative results started with a negative thought, not a negative action. So what was your negative thought?

Exercise 2 – Fix 2: The positive spiral

Look at your negative spiral and ask yourself: where does it all go wrong? What is the thought that allows the negative spiral to go out of control? By finding this thought you can make the decision to have a new thought. A positive one.

Now allow your mind to play with and daydream a positive spiral. What could that look like? Let's take the negative spiral above, and reverse it.

▶ You meet someone and you get talking and they like what you have to say. They ask you to send them an email outlining your ideas in more detail.

▶ You don't hear from them so, instead of making the assumption that they are not interested, you phone them to check they got your email. (You don't hide behind email, because you want an answer, right?)

▶ If you get an answerphone you email them, advising them that you will be in touch in a few days' time to get some feedback.

▶ You think how great it could be if it worked out. And that is the *big* difference. You think how great it could be.

> **"All too often we allow our minds to wander into a bad place and assume the worst. We never think the best is going to happen."**

All too often we allow our minds to wander into a bad place and assume the worst. We never think the best is going to happen.

Exercise 3 – The 'What if?' game

If you want success, then you need to start assuming it *could* happen. So, as you get to grips with controlling your negative spiral and readjusting the balance, start playing the 'What if?' game and list all the great things that could happen:

▶ What if they loved it and headhunted me?

▶ What if they want to roll it out to every branch in the country?

- What if I end up as CEO?
- What if this leads to my dream job?

"Why would you limit what you are capable of achieving?"

Go on, imagine you are 10 years old. Do you remember when you were 10 and someone asked you what you wanted to do when you grew up and you still thought it was perfectly reasonable to be an astronaut, pop star, vet and bed tester? (Well why not?) It is only by limiting your thoughts that you limit what you can create. So why would you limit what you are capable of achieving?

Exercise 4 – Play the crazy version of the 'What if?' game

Play the 'What if?' game and imagine the most amazing, far out, crazy, fantastic things happening. These things *do* happen to some people. Why not you? This is a new way of thinking what the 'What if?' game can help you access. Fear struggles to hide when you have fun. Make the game *beyond* fun. Make it silly.

Take the 'What if?' game one step too far. You see, fear doesn't cope well with being ridiculed. It relies on you accepting that it's real. Fear relies on you needing it. When you muck around and 'play daft' it gets cross and then you can see fear for what it really is. Something that is just in the way of your success. And when you can see something as an obstacle, you quickly work out how to get rid of it.

You can even get surreal. For instance, imagine the person that loved your idea phoned your office and said, 'Yes, it's *that* good we want you to take ownership of the company; we are going to throw in a bucket of puppies, a few private jets (full of kittens) and make you president of the world. Shall we knock up some bank notes with your face on now?'

"Too often we think small, restricting our goals and our ambitions."

It sounds silly, doesn't it? But just by making the game this daft, your brain starts to take some of the sting out of the fear for you. How can you fear succeeding if you think it's so daft? This game also allows you to expand the reach of your success. Too often we think small, restricting our goals and our ambitions. This crazy game enables you to think bigger than you would ever normally dare.

Exercise 5 – The 'What if?' game to destruction

Now you've played the 'What if?' game, you can appreciate the power of your thoughts over the actions you make, and how they can manipulate what you choose to do and how that impacts on your belief about your ability to achieve. What about taking that the other way? What about playing the 'What if?' game to destruction?

When I work with people that face a fear, it can help to deal with fears head on. We've all heard the saying 'What's the worst that can happen?' And, in fact, we probably don't think about the worst that could happen. About 75 per cent of the time, I would guess, people think about the most obvious negative thing that could happen. No one said it *would* happen. It's just easy to allow your brain to slip into negative thought. So what about taking that easy natural lapse one huge step forward?

Let's play the 'What if?' game to destruction and imagine the worst-case scenario.

▶ You meet someone and you get talking and they like what you have to say. They ask you to send them an email outlining your ideas in more detail.

▶ You don't hear from them so you make the assumption that they are not interested.

▶ You think you are a fool and that they know you are a fool too.

▶ You assume they've phoned your current boss/customers to tell them how rubbish you are and that they should get rid of you and never use you ever again.

▶ They post your picture on the 6 o'clock news and the news reporter is saying that you are public enemy number one and should not be engaged with, employed or talked to under any circumstances.

▶ You lose your home and your job and move to a cave of mud and live off rain water.

Now, that's a worst-case scenario.

Is this likely to happen? Of course not. However, it makes you challenge what you think right? Is it really likely they hate you? Is it really likely they are not interested? Or is it more likely that they are just busy and haven't had a chance to reply yet?

A – Actions

Assumptions

What assumption do you make when it comes to your ability to succeed?

▶ Do you assume your boss hates you?

▶ Do you assume your work colleagues dislike you?

▶ Do you assume your work is below standard?

▶ Do you assume you're rubbish at public speaking/new technology/ learning things?

▶ Do you assume people are talking about you? (In which case, Chapter 10 is important for you.)

▶ Do you assume people aren't interested because they didn't reply to your email or answerphone message the same day? Did you only receive two messages today? So why do you make the assumption that the other party is sat there with nothing to do?

> **"Assumptions are allowed to grow and manifest as ugly blights on our success, attacking our chances of winning at work."**

See how it works? We make assumptions that stack up in fear's favour to prove that our worse fears are true, and the assumptions are allowed to grow and manifest as ugly blights on our success, attacking our chances of winning at work. So stop the assumptions. Right now!

I find assumptions are so dangerous. They are fears waiting to manifest. Assumptions are like baby fears waiting to mutate into the fears you hide in your subconscious. So, what assumptions are you making? Assumptions and fear: a dangerous combination. And they are undermining your success rate, because you enable them to. You allow them to sneak in and whisper in your ear: 'Hey, you don't really think you can do that do you?'

Facts (the real ones)

Now we've played the 'What if?' game to get your brain thinking about what you choose to think, let's look at your facts:

▶ What is your basis for fact?

▶ Is your belief that you will fail rooted in fact?

▶ Have you always failed?

▶ What proof do you have?

There will be plenty of examples of actions you have taken, things you've done and achieved in your life where you have succeeded. *So write them down, remember them.* Know on a good day what will power up a bad day. And knowing what your successes are can really help when you're having a bad day. When you feel like things are failing, when your thoughts are overriding facts, it's important to remember the *real* facts and not let the false thoughts overpower the truth. That is when fear is allowed to work on your success.

We talked at the start of this chapter about too much talk. I do think there is too much talk in our society and it can really damage our success rate. We constantly compare ourselves to the person next to us, and what we are choosing to desire or achieve. Are we really successful? Are they more successful or am I? Who cares!

"Do not give in to the pressure to live up to someone else's version of life."

Start monitoring success according to your internal parameters, and not according to the person next to you. Do not give in to the pressure to live up to someone else's version of life:

▶ Would you go into a restaurant and eat what the guy in front had ordered, regardless?

▶ Would you walk into the airport and randomly put a pin in the board and say, 'That's my dream destination!'?

▶ Would you jump in the next car at the traffic lights and hope it got you to where you wanted to go?

Of course not; your destination is unique to you. Your life should mean something to you. So take some pressure off and stop looking over your shoulder. The fear that you will not succeed is compounded by the constant pressure of seeing what everyone else is achieving. 'Look what x has done'. 'Look where they went'. 'Look what contract they just got'. And remember, is every word posted online true? That fact seems to get forgotten when we are comparing ourselves to everyone else!

Influencers

I think a massive downside of our engaged and interactive life is that we know what everyone is doing all of the time. Thus I would like you to ask yourself:

▶ Am I influenced by what I read online?

▶ Do other people's viewpoints impact on my charity choices? On my holiday choices? On my clothing? On my eating habits? On my leisure activities? On the way I conduct business?'

▶ Do I feel that my own voice is still heard or do I wonder what my own voice sounds like in there?

If you measure your life against everyone else's, how can you know if you are getting the results you want? Or do you just use other people as a good guide so you feel comfortable and reassured in your own goals and ambitions?

"If you measure your life against everyone else's, how can you know if you are getting the results you want?"

If you feel pressurised into what you write online and/or what you think, is it time to consider the impact that the world around you is having on your success? You can remove a lot of stress and pressure if you are aware of the goals and ambitions you are looking to achieve and not considering what other people think of the goals that you are choosing to set for yourself.

Imagine you were looking to lose weight. If you did this in a group, could those around you influence you into or out of action? It is the same when it comes to the limitations you create for your own success. *Does the world around you empower your belief about success, or create non-existent obstacles?*

It's important to consider who influences your life. One of the best things I do for my business success is network. It's not just about creating new business and staying on people's radar for new opportunities, it ensures I keep my mindset powered up and positive. When our heads are down and we are intent on the prize it can be all too easy to get so caught up with the end result that we lose track of how we are going to get there. In Chapter 4 we will look at this area in more detail. However, for now consider:

▶ Who do you surround yourself with?

▶ What people do you allow to influence your success?

▶ What impact do the people in your professional life have on your success?

▶ What impact do the people in your personal life have on your ability to win at work?

Because maybe you want success and yet you wobble in your belief that you can achieve. Are the people around you powering up your chances of success or powering up your fears?

 # R – Results

I like to share the story of Mary Anning, a 12-year-old anthropologist from the 19th century who I'd found out about on a day out with my family in Cambridge recently. Mary was part of a working-class family who appreciated that fossils carried a value and so she started to collect them to sell. She turned an interest in collecting into a way of feeding her family, and that led to a business. And she went on to have a reputable career in the industry, despite it being rather unheard of for a young woman. (Remember at the time women in the UK did not even have the vote.) Do you think Mary was looking around her thinking, 'I wonder what Martha down the road is doing?' I added to the image of Mary Anning a rather flippant comment. I wrote 'Mary was awesome. Mary started being awesome at 12. Mary didn't think "today I will be awesome". Mary got on with stuff! Successful people get on with the right stuff.'

And I wouldn't mind betting that, despite my flippancy, Mary also didn't worry about whether she would be successful. Mary just got on with what she was doing, because that was what she felt needed to be done. It was the necessary course of action. And it felt like the necessary course of action because Mary concentrated on what Mary was doing rather than what Martha or anyone else was doing. When I was one of the UK's youngest automotive body shop managers, I don't think that on any day of my career I ever got up and contemplated about that thought. I just got up and got on with running across the workshop working out what size bolt was needed to get the car out to the customer!

I think the ethos of the Nike company has never been more true: 'Just do it'. And, in a world of motivational sayings on social media, we need a little less talk and a little more action. Be more like Mary Anning and worry less about *thinking* about doing it and worry more about *doing* it.

"In a world of motivational sayings on social media, we need a little less talk and a little more action."

Remember:

▶ The 'What if?' game.

▶ The negative spiral.

▶ The positive spiral.

And if you are really feeling the fear take the 'What if?' game to extremes and let your own subconscious take the pain out of the fear. (Remember fear hates it when you laugh at it.)

Be like the client that played the 'What if?' game to destruction and contemplated the big goals; by dreaming big and going for it, they would in fact lose their loved ones, because they would hate them for working all day and all night, and they laughed so much they realised it was ridiculous because their family had been so supportive of their work-related goals. It helped them see that if they wanted to achieve more they just had to share those goals with the people they loved and they could then start to look at the ways to achieve them. They could also be a great role model for other members of the family too.

So your fear of succeeding could turn into a powerful motivator for more people than just you. Now that is a brilliant outcome!

CHAPTER

4

I don't want to appear arrogant

F – Fear

Often when I'm working with a client, as we get closer to understanding what stands in the way of winning results, it really does hit them with a shock that fear is impacting them. And I want to help you find the fear that is in the way of your success.

One of the fears that likes to hide out and manifest as so many other negative results in our lives is the fear of not wanting to look arrogant.

Again you may be reading this thinking, 'This really doesn't apply to me'. So ask yourself right now, 'How would I feel if I was considered the very pinnacle of exceptional skill, talent and professionalism for my industry?' Would that sit comfortably for you? Does it make you smile? Or is there a little element of cringing niggly fear that you can't put your finger on?

If you were to explore that feeling a bit more, would you be able to find a lot of negativity? Possibly a good few excuses as to how it couldn't work? How would your life need to change to be able to achieve that high position? Do you feel you aren't ready yet or don't have the experience yet? Do you feel that there are a lot of restrictions on your time and commitments that you have to look after?

Excuses are a good sign to me that someone is getting close to what they really want. The excuses come out when we are scared. 'Yes I want it, but . . . ' The 'but' is big, because, well let's be honest, it's scary right? And boom, there's a fear!

> **"Excuses are a good sign to me that someone is getting close to what they really want."**

Not all fears make you wake in the night dripping with sweat and wanting the light left on. Some hide: we answer everyone's comments on Facebook or send out emails rather than phoning because we are too frightened to actually stand up high on the top of the castle's biggest tower and shout 'This is me and I'm awesome at what I do!'

Ok, so I'm not asking you to start walking down the street doing that (for many reasons!) However, I am asking you to change what you think. Because the fear of looking arrogant shoves people so far away from the tallest tower of the castle of success that they end up hanging out in the servants' quarters, hiding behind email and other people's accolades for the rest of their lives. It's scary to say 'I'm great at what I do'. This is not arrogance; this is quiet confidence.

When people give me the excuses and the reasons why it couldn't be them to make it, I feel a quiet bit of excitement, because it's highly likely we are finding the goals that really matter to that person. Remember we said how the things in life need to make you feel a certain way? Well, when the excuses start, I know we are getting to the heart of what matters to that person. I don't want to look at the excuses; as humans we can justify any and every action we take. We can talk ourselves into and out of everything and anything. What I want to do is help you understand that you are *choosing* to step away from the precipice of success for fear of getting too close. You are only too close if you are heading over the side and *that* area is arrogance; anything *before* is confidence. That is how you define the difference between arrogance and confidence. The top is a good place. You just have to fight the fear to get there.

> **"The top is a good place. You just have to fight the fear to get there."**

The reason that you need to master the skill of quiet confidence is that to succeed and get the results you want, and to overcome the fears that damage success, you need to be able to draw on that inner confidence. That inner confidence will be the voice that says 'Why not me?' instead of 'What makes you think they want you?' or 'What makes you think you are good enough?'

One of the reasons we don't let our brilliance shine is because we really don't want to look arrogant. It's a fear that so many have of looking big headed. How many times have you heard 'No one likes a show off'? It's what your mum used to say when, as a child, someone wheelied up the street on their bike. And that sentence was normally followed by, 'They will come a cropper'. In other words, they will hurt themselves. So our mind says, 'Whoa don't go around telling everyone you are brilliant because then you are at risk of "coming a cropper"', and that leads to failure. And if you think a fear of arrogance is big, you've seen nothing until you've seen a fear of failure.

 # E – Examples and exercises

Firstly, let's look at arrogance. We've all had to endure a person with the subtlety of a brick who has a way of creating an atmosphere that makes everyone in the room feel uncomfortable, because to them everyone else is a lesser being compared to them. They are someone that has no idea that they are making everyone wish they were elsewhere (even the dentist's chair!) because this person's persona is being rammed down everyone's oesophagus.

We are so scared of being like this person that we act the complete opposite and hide the fabulousness of who we are. You may think that is a superficial, 'girlie' comment, but every time I've made anyone, male or female, do the exercises in this chapter it has created the same results.

Example 1

A business owner told me how they had big ambitions for their company, and together we planned them out. We broke them down into years and months, and into weekly goals. We looked for the pitfalls and the beliefs. As we worked together something became very clear they had a strong belief that was heavily impacting on their success rate, regardless of their ability to retain staff, gain new customers or have a social life.

They believed it was arrogant for them to assume that they could stand head and shoulders above their competitors. They said to me 'Who am I to say that we are better than anyone else?' I won't divulge what we discussed. However, the tools for results are in this chapter, along with some great little games that you can use to trick your mind back into positive thought and real results. Cool, right?

Our brains are sneaky toads at the best of times. Just as you think you've got a handle on what you are thinking, you will find you are walking into something new or a little different and you will become aware of a new thought. As you play with it, it becomes pliable like putty in your hands, and if you have really listened to this book, you will stop your thoughts in their tracks and say 'Whoa, hold on there, this thought is not helping me!' And that's what I want to see happening for you in this chapter. When the business owner questioned 'Why us?' I asked 'Why not you?'

Example 2

I was once in a room full of business owners, discussing their start-up businesses. One of the business owners was asking me how to get their business seen online. We were discussing how they needed to stand out – which is, in essence, what this chapter is about. You need to have the confidence to stand up and be you. To step up and have the confidence to say 'I'm awesome'. This business owner said, 'But what we do, so many other businesses do too, so how do we stand out in a market like that?'

❝You need to have the confidence to stand up and be you. To step up and have the confidence to say 'I'm awesome'.❞

I went on to explain how to stand out and the business owner looked horrified. 'But if we do that we are pretty much saying we are the best aren't we?' I asked them 'Do you not think you are?' Why would you set up your own business if you didn't think you could deliver something exceptional to people? Who sets up their own business and thinks 'Mmmm I bet I can do a half-hearted job and get paid a mediocre wage for it'? This is why defining your version of confidence and stepping away from the fear of arrogance is so important.

Exercise 1 – 'Why I'm awesome' two-page document

You need to re-train your brain. I don't want to push you over the edge into arrogance, I just want to take you to the right side of 'I'm fabulous'.

Be aware: this exercise has been used with corporate business men and women who have looked down their noses at me, probably thinking 'I paid you to help me be more successful and this is what you will have me do!' And yet sometimes, as quickly as within a day, they come back to me saying 'Okay I get it'. And when I see them next, just this one exercise has changed the way they look, their actions and their very mannerisms!

Fear lurks, it doesn't always jump out at you and grip you in a vice. Sometimes it's just out of sight. And when I'm working with a client, I can watch someone physically change the way they sit. Their bodies give away what they are thinking and feeling long before their words do. This exercise is a good way of helping you to get your mind back on side and expose what you really think. It can help you to appreciate how much skill, expertise and brilliance you already have. As humans we are always striving for more, which in so many ways is great. However, the downside of this is that we don't stop to appreciate how good we already are.

❝As humans we are always striving for more. The downside of this is that we don't stop to appreciate how good we already are.❞

So many times I've changed a person's mindset in less than an hour, just by helping them reframe their attitude to who they already are at this moment in time. Before you start looking at what you need to change, what you need to develop and work on, look at what is already rather awesome.

I want you to write, with old fashioned pen and paper, a two-page A4 list of why you are awesome. What results do you get?

▶ **Good results?** For some people this is easy. It rolls out of their mind and on to the paper with no effort. The pages will be full in minutes. (If that's the case, are they really the things you are most proud of? Do they really define the things you want to stand up and be known for around the world?)

▶ **Bad results?** If you struggle to find two pages of awesomeness, dig deeper. You see, in my experience we rarely see what other people see. We are the world's worst at accepting compliments, dismissing them and knocking them aside as if they never happened. Try and remember every compliment you've been given, from the compliment on your outfit, to the nice comments on that report you wrote.

It's always fascinated me how, if you are good at something, you assume that everyone else is good at it too. On the other hand, if you are not good at something you berate yourself for being stupid and assume the rest of the world are experts at it. Why are we so hard on ourselves?

Still struggling? If you want lasting success, you need to learn to hear compliments, and the first person you need to hear them from is yourself. So think:

▶ What moments in your life are you proud of?
▶ Did you plan a wedding and have everyone say it was the best day of their lives?
▶ Did you have the best adventure on holiday?

These things didn't happen by accident; you put the trip together, you planned it, you took action and made it happen. How did you make it special? Those are some of the skills that you need to get on your two-page list. Because if you don't say nice things to yourself, why should anyone else?

"If you don't say nice things to yourself, why should anyone else?"

Becoming more aware of what your internal voice is saying means that you can actually get a word in edgeways and say the *right* things to yourself. Ask yourself this: 'If I agree to say the wrong things to myself then what am I agreeing to?' How could your thoughts be impacting on your actions and your results at work? And if that doesn't rocket you into action, ask yourself 'Am I really prepared to say the wrong things to myself and stop myself from winning at work?'

Remember how we talked about having a strong enough desire to take action? How a goal should make you feel giddy with excitement and make you think 'Wow, yes, let's do this!' Asking these questions should cause you enough pain to make you ask yourself 'why would I accept anything less than what I want in life?'

When you have your two-page list of why you are awesome, remember you are not suddenly going to start walking into the office or the local store and shaking people's hand saying 'Hello my name's X and I'm awesome'. Now, that would be arrogance! This is about creating quiet internal confidence that keeps you strong and powerful. So when things go wrong – and, let's be honest, the happiest, most wonderful lives still have things go wrong – you will have the inner confidence in yourself, your skills and experiences to say 'It's all good'.

Exercise 2 – The arrogant me game

As you build your confidence, it's all too easy that the fear of arrogance will sneak back. You could find yourself second-guessing choices, wondering whether you should 'go for it'. You can play this game to find out if you really have anything to worry about.

1 Imagine what an arrogant version of you would look like. Take it to a silly level. Make a version of you that is practically a caricature.

2 See yourself walking into work and shouting loudly 'Good morning everyone, please don't forget I'm gorgeous and better at everything than you!' See yourself strutting through the building, swaggering like something off of a catwalk with a look that says 'I'm better than anyone on this planet'. Heck, say that out loud to everyone in the room. Now does *that* sound and *feel* ridiculous?

When we experience fear, sometimes we can bring ourselves back to a more productive way of thinking by just being silly. The next time you worry that you are too close to the precipice and fearful of telling someone that they should recruit you for the job, or give you that big opportunity, play the above game and imagine the worst, most arrogant version of you in that scenario. You will be able to see that you are a million miles away from being anything other than fabulous. Remember this is about fighting fear to get what you want, and you have to get yourself on your side.

"Remember this is about fighting fear to get what you want, and you have to get yourself on your side. "

Now how will you know that you have achieved quiet confidence? What does quiet confidence look like to you?

A – Action

When you work with a coach, you have someone there that will confront and challenge you in the beliefs that damage success. They will hunt out the fears that you didn't even know existed and help you question your own thinking, so that you can see the damage your negative thoughts can have on your actions and, ultimately, results.

If you can't have a coach there every day, then you to need to work on getting your confidence levels in order. Practise as much care, attention to detail and kindness to your mindset as you would to your teeth, your hair or any other part of your body. It is belief of mine that we spend so much time looking after our bodies yet we rarely check the quality of our thoughts. And yet if your thoughts are not positively charged, they can damage the results of your actions.

"We spend so much time looking after our bodies yet we rarely check the quality of our thoughts. "

If you want greater odds of winning at work then you need to have an internal belief in yourself that takes you to the right side of confidence. For instance:

Do you have a big meeting today? = What was the last thought you let wander through your mind before you left the house?

Are you faced with a new challenge today? = What do you believe about your ability compared to that of your work colleagues or competitors?

Watch out for these actions that you may have taken in the past. Here are some ideas as to how to deal with them from today:

Someone asks if you know anyone that can deliver training on X; you recommend a competitor or colleague.	You appreciate that you have these skills, although you have not delivered training. However, you have sat in on enough training courses, and have enough transferable skills to be able to learn to do a great job at this.
You are in a meeting and they look for someone to lead a project. Everyone knows the people that are good at it, and it's not you.	You would love the chance. You know this project is coming to the table so you work out your natural talents, plan how you will confidently share your intent to be heavily involved, and your aim to lead this project. If not this one, the next!
Being a thought leader and standing up and saying 'I know what I'm talking about' is big headed and there are so many people that know more about this than I do.	Someone has to be the expert, and when I write down how many years' experience I have, how many books I've read, how much I've invested in this work, how much I've spent on this profession, I appreciate that I too am an expert. That does not take away from other experts, it just raises me to the same standard as them. I've every right to be seen as a thought leader in my industry.

So what thoughts are you going to allow to power up your mind? By reframing your thoughts, and being aware of your natural tendency to shy away for fear of being arrogant, you will be able to feel naturally confident in your own worth and be at the top of your confidence castle without going near the dangerous depths of arrogance, and that is seriously good for winning at work!

 # R – Result

I was speaking with a successful photographer who I'd worked with, and they were saying how they didn't feel nervous when they went to a new venue or an event for a client any more. I asked them why, and you could see this person really thinking about their reply. They realised it was inner confidence. That they knew they were good at what they did, they knew how to deliver and that a new environment was not to be feared – it was to be welcomed. This would be hard to do if this photographer didn't have inner confidence in themselves. And the fact that they were sharing this with me showed that they were indeed confident and nowhere near arrogant. It was that quiet pat on the back that said, 'Yes, I'm capable and exceptional at what I do'. And not once did I feel anything other than absolute happiness for this person. *That* is confidence.

If you don't think you are brilliant, why should anyone else? If you don't speak up confidently and positively about yourself, why should anyone else? Can you see how that could impact on your success?

I have said this to a good few clients over the years. Without the right mindset you are like a Ferrari that you intend to run on milk. You look great, but you aren't going anywhere. Power up your results today, by thinking the right thoughts. And that starts with quiet confidence. Get your inner coach onside. You *can* do it, you *will* do it and you *will* be awesome. You have a two-page A4 page document that proves it, right?

CHAPTER

5

I don't ask for help

F – Fear

'Big deal', you say. 'I don't need to ask for help, so what? It's hardly a fear! It's just me being brilliant, organised and awesome getting to where I want to be, right?' . . . or something along those lines. Well if that's the case, why is this a chapter that I feel practically wrote itself!

Here are some common beliefs:

▶ 'If someone helps me get to where I want to be then that undermines my achievements.'

▶ 'If someone helps me to get the results I want then I'm weak. Why couldn't I achieve them on my own?'

▶ 'No one can ever know that I don't know how to get to where I want to be and that I'm struggling; if they find out I will get eaten alive!'

▶ 'I can't ask for help! How stupid will people think I am if I couldn't get this done on my own? Everyone else copes!'

And so on and so on. Sorry to depress you while you read folks, but we live in a world where mental health illnesses are on the increase; where alcohol is poured as a pick-me-up throughout the week and chocolate is handed out as a fix it all, and we are becoming a world of over needy 'pat on the back' adrenalin junkies OD-ing on motivational messages. Yet stress is causing work-related absences. People are addicted to their phones and cannot physically leave them behind for a meal, let alone a holiday (more of that in Chapter 12). And life has never been more difficult to handle.

The human being is not a striped hog-nosed skunk. 'I know that Mandie', you say! The difference between a human and a striped hog-nosed skunk is that the striped hog-nosed skunk can happily live in isolation its whole life, until it needs to do the necessary. It likes a solitary life. As can the dusky footed woodrat. But the human, not so much. Think back to the caveman paintings. Ever see the caveman sat on his own? Did the caveman happily forage alone? Of course not! The caveman did not become the human that lives in civilisation today because he went out to hunt a mammoth alone. He needed other humans. Humans are *not* solitary creatures!

By our very nature, by our very creation, we are meant to work together and yet we think success is supposed to be a dish that can only be served alone. And that leads to a ridiculous level of fear and negative results in our success at work.

> **"By our very nature, by our very creation, we are meant to work together."**

It can lead to us feeling overloaded and unable to cope. That is a fear that manifests itself in a different way. Instead of a full-blown attack of fright, it's a fear that hunts you down, constantly berates you and reminds you that everyone else is good enough. It's just *you* that can't do it alone. It's just *you* that fails. It's just *you* that's inadequate. *Everyone else* is capable of doing the long days, the tough commute, the busy lives, it's just *you* that can't do it. Just *you*.

When you read this now you can probably see how crazy it sounds. However, the fact is that we rarely hold up our hands and say 'No actually this is *hard!* I need some help!' And it really needs the exclamation marks, because instead of thinking things out logically and working out our goals and planning them step by step, so that you can see well in advance the stages at which you could need more help and the stages when you will be able to get on with it alone, we leave it to build up until we feel totally overwhelmed and its only *then*, when we're about ready to snap, scream, cry or kick something, that we say '*No I can't do this alone!*' That is a sneaky evil fear. That is a fear that not only damages your success, it whittles away your confidence, your self-esteem and even your ability to believe you can succeed!

The first thing I want you to do when it comes to dealing with the fear of asking for help is to accept that it is a thing. Shall we kick it?

E – Examples and exercises

Examples

I speak from experience here. Learning to get over the fear of asking for help was one of the hardest lessons I learnt in business, and it was so often offered. (I was just never prepared to notice it!) I assumed it was offered because people thought I was incapable. On the contrary, people thought I was so capable, they wanted the opportunity to work alongside me, to learn something and to help me. Another reason people offered is because *they just wanted to help me*. There was no hidden agenda, no attempt to undermine my career, or take my promotion. It was just genuine kindness, just wanting to see me finish work at a decent hour. For me, my instant thought had been (which I share honestly and openly with you) that the person offering help wanted to take something from me or that they were trying to ruin my success. And, in fact, this spoke far less about them, and far more about me. It spoke about my vulnerability, not about their intentions. And in this chapter I will share the tools and techniques that I utilised to get over it and win at work.

Exercise 1 – Automatic response

To find out how the fear of saying no impacts on you, ask yourself if you are able to accept help. Or do you think, 'I'm fine thanks, I've got this covered'/'I can handle this'. It's a phrase that falls out of our mouths so fast sometimes it's hit our ears before we've registered we've said it. And we so wish we hadn't!

This is the thing to say, right? I can handle this? Of course I can! It's the standard response to the question 'How are you?' . . . 'I'm good thanks, you?' See? No thought, just instant reply. So let's look at the emotions behind the reason why we say these things:

▶ You worry what people will think.

▶ Depending on who asked, it could be you don't want to put them out.

▶ You don't want to cause them work.

▶ Maybe you don't want them to respect you less.

▶ You don't want them to steal your praise.

▶ You don't want to let people down.

Have you considered that they want to help you because it's their chance to do something for you?

Exercise 2 – Negative spiral time

When you think of someone offering help, how does it make you feel? Are you comfortable with it? Are there some people that you wouldn't accept help from and others that you would? What reasons could there be for that? By answering these questions in your head for a moment you might find you begin to understand yourself a little better.

As you take the fear of the asking for help further, think back to the negative spiral. Imagine playing out a negative spiral here. I've used this with enough clients to know it's a powerful tool to help you really understand the damage that not asking for help can do to your success. And, worse still, the power you can be giving to fear. If you assist fear today, you are helping it grow for tomorrow too. That's scary, right?

Allow the negative spiral to play out in your head now. Think about a time when you wanted to achieve a lot and you were up against it. Maybe you had a big deadline, maybe things were going wrong. Did you ask for help? Would things have been easier if you had?

It's not easy to ask for help, and at this stage I'm not asking you to imagine that you fixed it. I'm just asking you to think of the feeling of relief that you could have felt if you had known you were sharing the burden with someone else. I've a feeling your shoulders might have dropped, you may have sighed with relief and there may even have been room in your head to think 'right, I think I may have space to work out how to achieve this with two pairs of hands and two brains working through to get the solutions we need'. (I only work in solutions, rarely problems.)

" Think of the feeling of relief that you could have felt if you had known you were sharing the burden with someone else. "

You see, success really is achieved when you ask for help. And if you realise as you read this that your success is being hampered by not asking for help, it's probably a very real possibility you need to play out a negative spiral.

Power up your negative spiral to appreciate the results you are choosing to get:

▶ What is the likely course of events when you do everything yourself?
▶ What does that lead to?
▶ What does that then mean?
▶ What results does that create?
▶ What does that then mean?
▶ How does that then make you feel?
▶ What actions does that mean that you take?
▶ Then what do you do?
▶ What does that mean that you do?

And so on.

It's highly likely you are creating a downward spiral that leaves you feeling trapped, out of control and overburdened. You feel like everyone puts on you. And when you feel negative emotions, you are more likely to create negative actions. And negative actions create negative results. And do negative results lead to winning at work? Or do they lead to more fear and more failure? Do they lead to more feelings and limiting thoughts of 'I can't do this'? or 'I don't win'. Ask yourself when you get overloaded. When you don't ask for help, what emotions do you feel?

I hear a lot of business owners and people striving for success saying to me 'I can't trust anyone else to get it right'. Let's look at this shall we?

First of all, if you don't allow someone else to do some of the work, then what are you agreeing to? The answer is above – it's a negative spiral that results in all the negatives you get in your life. I want you to really *feel* it. Really intensify your pain level. I want you to feel so uncomfortable about your negative spiral that you literally are moving in your seat, physically squirming! When I'm working with a client, I use questions like the ones above to help the client really feel the pain. Because when you are so aware of what you are doing to yourself that it feels embarrassing and uncomfortable, you will do anything to get away from it.

Think about this now. This is an actual exercise. You may have a grip on life and say 'I don't need any help at all at the moment'; however, everyone has moments in their life where they need a little help, and it is far better to know and appreciate how you will accept that proffered help today than when your head is buzzing with hassles, problems and deadlines.

"Everyone has moments in their life where they need a little help."

Take a moment to think 'What do I need to do or think to ensure that, if and when I need help, I make sure I accept it and allow that person to do what I want them to do, so that I create the mental space to enable me to power up my success?' Remember if you don't create a solution for this, what are you agreeing to? Are you agreeing that whenever there is too much on your desk or your proverbial plate of life that you have to be stressed, overworked, screaming or crying on the inside and wondering why is life so hard, thinking 'How will I get through this?' What impact could that have on your success? Therefore, it's better to take a moment to think this one through, right?

If it feels like a big deal to you that someone else comes in and steals your thunder, start small. Don't give anyone mountains of your work. Just ask for the tiniest of help. Maybe ask for help with something that you could actually do in your sleep. But think about this: if they are doing some of the jobs that you can do easily, does that not mean you have a bit of brain space to concentrate on the other things that are whirring and whizzing around in your overworked brain?

We've looked at why you should ask for help. We've looked at how you ask for help. However, I think it's also important to look at how it makes you *feel*. It's important that you really learn to reframe the thoughts you have associated with asking for help so that the fear is quashed for good. Look for every negative connotation that you associate with asking for help. Every negative thought needs replacing with a positive one. For instance:

Negative thought	Becomes	Positive thought
Asking for help is a sign weakness	⟶	Asking for help is of a sign of strength in my own self.

List the negatives of asking for help. Then list the positives of asking for help. These could include, although are not limited to:

▶ It's weak to ask for help.

▶ They will steal my great ideas and get my opportunities for themselves.

▶ It shows a lack of organisation.

▶ Asking for help is lame.

▶ Asking for help makes you look incapable.

▶ I'm not a child, I'm a grown up, I should be able to cope.

▶ Successful people do it alone; they don't ask for help.

▶ I don't want people to think I'm stupid.

▶ I could lose my job.

▶ People could laugh at me.

And so on and so on. Write as many negative ideas you can associate with asking for help. Really get to the bottom of why it's such a bad idea to ask for assistance. It's good to do this at this stage in the chapter because, despite having the evidence that says why you should, you will still be able to justify why you shouldn't ask for help. (I've always loved the way a client can justify why they can or cannot do something! And I love the way, with the right conversation, we can work together to get that Eureka moment that shifts their thoughts into a more constructive way of thinking!) So let's challenge your thinking right now.

Write your long negative list. Tell me why it's such a bad idea to ask for help. Now let's flip that on its head. How long a list can you create here?

Positives of asking for help:

▶ I free up my brain space to concentrate on bigger things.
▶ I play to my strengths and accept my weaknesses as areas to improve or things to accept.
▶ I know what I want to achieve and that's what matters.
▶ People respect my determination to get results.
▶ It shows confidence in oneself to be able to ask for help.

Successful people rely on the right teams and support. In all organisations, even in the animal kingdom, everyone works on what they are good at to ensure the ultimate success of the community.

" In all organisations, even in the animal kingdom, everyone works on what they are good at to ensure the ultimate success of the community. "

By asking for help, I can get more done in one day. I can get more goals achieved faster because I'm able to work smarter. Our 21st-century success is about thinking in a strategic way, that means I'm comfortable being honest about the person I am.

What will appear on your positive list to ensure you know how to accept help to achieve lasting success? What will make you challenge your thinking? What do you need to remember? What are your 'why's? Remember the goals you want to achieve and that we planned together in Chapter 2. Remember that by giving into the negative fear of saying 'Yes', you are agreeing to letting your success slide away too. It's worth accepting that help now, right?

A – Actions

The problem that so many of us have is that we fight on like superheroes, yet we aren't superhuman. Please remember this, *you are not superhuman*. You can't zap your way to a deadline or mind meld your boss into giving you a promotion.

However, you do have one superhuman power: you can power up the use of your brain from this moment in time, even though you don't actually have the ability to do everything on your own without risking overload. Or, worse still, you can cause physical damage to your body, sleepless nights, arguments with your family and much more. The repercussions for you and the ones you love and care about can be far reaching; this fear can impact on more than just your ability to win at work. So it's a good idea to get the superhuman power of your brain into action, right? We tell ourselves all the time that we will work harder to get to the ultimate prize; however, time and time again studies show us that we work far harder to get away from the pain and the fear.

Think about it: pain or pleasure?

Pain	Pleasure
You work harder and faster to get to your goal when you are near a deadline and you don't want your boss to see you've not finished.	You were never motivated by the joy of seeing your boss's happy face when you hand the finished work in.
You work hard to slim down in time for the school reunion to confront the bully from 20 years ago.	You enjoy the smug feeling when you saunter in looking good in front of the bully that made your life a misery for seven years.
You actually steer clear of social media to get your work done when the deadline is tomorrow.	You enjoy the pat on the back you give yourself for a job well done.

See, we are motivated by pain. I've done enough successful marketing campaigns to know this! So really feel your pain, so that you feel silly for *not* asking for help in all these years. Feel it like a physical thing, as if it's in the room calling you rude names.

What does it mean you are agreeing to? It means you are agreeing to limiting your success. It means you are agreeing to damaging your health, agreeing to sleepless nights, rows with your loved ones, swearing at the cat or just not getting the results you want in your professional life. It means agreeing to the fears that impact on success.

Start small. If you are so habitually used to doing it all yourself, you may not be the kind of person that can just change overnight. That's fine.

Your natural style

As with everything you wish to achieve in life, you need to go at a pace that suits you. And when you work in accordance with your personality (and not according to some universal measure online or in the media!) then you will get lasting results. Thus we need to identify your natural style. How do you naturally get things done? What is the natural way you make things happen? (and don't worry if you are thinking 'I don't make it happen!' That is still a style!).

> **"When you work in accordance with your personality, you will get lasting results."**

To identify your natural style, we need to find out what kind of person you are. Are you the kind of person that, after being told that coffee is making your teeth go black, you stop drinking it that day, never to touch it ever again?

▶ Yes, you have a killer headache for a couple of days, and yes you miss it, but you get told to stop so you do.

Or

▶ You're the kind of person that says 'No! It's my coffee! Don't take my coffee! I can't do this! How will I cope?' and you don't take any action at all.

Or

▶ You are somewhere in the middle.

Please note I deliberately chose an example that is not work related. Your natural style will permeate through every part of your life. There may be other areas of your life where you allow it to show more; however, you will naturally choose to act in a certain way at all times. Even if you are with a group of people that all act a different way and you are forced to act according to them, you will still display characteristics of your natural style. We are creatures of habit!

So what is your natural style? Once again, using the coffee example:

▶ Would you give up from that moment?
▶ Would you wean yourself off?
▶ Would you create a spread sheet or a mindmap?
▶ Would you need to talk to someone about it?
▶ Would you post your goal on social media to ensure you did it and create momentum?

Now is a really good time to think about your natural style. Do you need to write a list? If you are giving up coffee do you need to get support? Do you need to go and buy 37 herbal teas to get you through and research online how to give up coffee? Are you a thinker or a doer? By knowing your natural style, you are able to bring that back to your ability to ask for help and think 'okay so if I'm not good at asking for help, do I start small or go large?'

▶ Do I start by taking on a housekeeper so I can concentrate on my career and business goals?

▶ Do I just need to accept that offer from my partner to cook dinner?

▶ Do you need to vocalise your need for help? (That in itself can be a massive obstacle).

Think about it. When I asked you at the start of the chapter how comfortable do you feel about asking people for help, were there people that you wouldn't ask for help? So, of the ones that you could, will you? What will you say? You don't need to write a script; however, answer these questions:

▶ How will I word my request to them?

▶ Do I need to formally arrange a meeting or will I just bring it up the next time I see them?

In this way, you can start to think about the reality of asking for help.

So, the next step comes when the offer is actually offered. How will you stand back and let it happen? I can *tell* you what to do. However, what are you going to do so that you challenge *yourself* to act in a different way from today? How will you ensure that when you need help, you accept that you are going to ask for it, and you work out how you are going to get it, you make sure you actually step back and let that help actually happen? Do you need to physically step away? Or will it be enough to remind yourself of this chapter and acknowledge that, by accepting the help, you are agreeing to power up your success, and eradicate the fear that asking for help is an admission of inferiority, inability or incapability?

R – Results

When this fear has manifested itself in a client's success I have often had someone sit before me and want to dismiss what I'm saying. And then, as I've laid out the actions they've been taking and as we've looked at the way they've been feeling and where it all started, they've had that little sparkle in their eye and had that real Eureka moment.

When I researched this chapter I found it hard to think of one person that had achieved it all on their own. Did Richard Branson do it alone? Even when I think back to how incredibly hard my father worked, did he do it on his own? No, of course not. He had my mother there, and together they were a team. He couldn't have done it without her. And although it's been a conversation around the family dinner table for years; all jokes aside, we've always been in agreement that great success comes from team work. And I couldn't be a success if I didn't have the support of my husband and other key people. I couldn't think of *one* person that has achieved success alone.

The biggest names in music had managers that were like their right arms. Mohandas K. Gandhi may have been the wisdom and taken the first steps, but it was a mass movement of thousands, and Mother Teresa inspired millions, but did she do it alone? No matter where I looked, I couldn't find one person who achieved great things, great success, lasting true success, alone.

❝I couldn't find one person who achieved great things, great success, lasting true success, alone.❞

Does the cross-channel swimmer do it alone? You could argue they do. However, they always have a support boat. They even have someone smear on the goose fat, otherwise they can't see through their goggles to see where they're going!

I saw one business owner take on a few key personnel when, only the year before, they'd happily bragged that they could 'do it all'. Their business was suddenly gaining contracts that could only have been dreamed of prior to this. Overcoming the fear of asking for help literally took their business to the next level. Overcome your fear of asking for help; appreciate that great success and winning at work is far more likely to be on the agenda if you fight this fear.

6

I'm scared of saying 'No'

F – Fear

Unless you have a 1-, 5- and 10-year plan for success that you are incredibly focused on, it's all too easy to slip into the habit of saying 'Yes' to every opportunity and every request that comes your way. 'What's wrong with that?' I hear you say. Nothing, as long as you intend to stick around on this planet for about 250 years!

The Catherine wheel effect

I've seen so many fabulously talented people struggle to get the results they want, and all because they have a habit of saying 'Yes' to everything. By doing this, you can end up creating the 'Catherine wheel' effect: you do a bit over here, and a bit over there and then another bit over there and then something else over here, and none of it really has any real momentum or power. The Catherine wheel looks pretty, but it doesn't do a lot of damage to your fence post!

Imagine if you took that Catherine wheel off and aimed it at your fence. What would happen then? You would likely end up with a hole in your fence, right? Focus is needed. Saying 'No' is necessary, but how do you work out what you say 'No' to?

Many of us fear saying 'No' because we wonder 'What will people think if I don't do it? We are a team, and how does this make me look if I don't do this?'

And what about the 'can you just-ers'? They always happen to have the tiniest of favours that need doing (usually on a Friday around 4.45 pm). How can you say 'No' to them? Won't that damage your career and your success?

There are, in fact, many times that the successful person learns to say 'No', but we are going to look at *why* they have learnt the power of that two-letter word (and, wow, is it powerful!) and how they say it.

> **‘‘When you don't say 'No' it can damage your chances of winning, and of achieving success, as well as getting the results you want. ’’**

First, let's look at the impact that the fear of saying 'No' can have on your success. When you don't say 'No' to anyone it can damage your chances of winning, of achieving success, as well as getting the results you want. When you constantly say 'Yes' to everyone you can become overloaded and, as we learnt in Chapter 5, becoming overburdened can damage more than just your success, it can damage your health too. It can impact on your loved ones and every aspect of your life. Therefore, if you want to increase your chances of success, you need to deal with the fear of saying 'No'.

So, ask yourself this (it's your choice if you write your thoughts down or just take a moment to think about this): 'By constantly saying "Yes", what am I agreeing to?' This could include (but is not limited to):

▶ I'm agreeing to not meeting my own deadlines.

▶ I'm agreeing to working a longer day.

▶ I'm agreeing to feeling tired and stressed.

▶ I'm agreeing to not having time to cook an evening meal/read to my children/watch TV with my partner.

▶ I'm agreeing to being too tired to read and falling asleep after the first three sentences.

▶ I'm agreeing to feeling resentful of that person who always gets me to finish their work because they can't do the job.

▶ I'm agreeing to hating that person because they get paid more than me and I get no recognition.

▶ I'm agreeing to feeling my success is less important than other people around me.

▶ I'm agreeing to fail.

"*It's a two-letter word that so many people struggle to use for fear of the repercussions.*"

Wow, doesn't it read like a scary list? And all for a two-letter word. And yet, it's a two-letter word that so many people struggle to use for fear of the repercussions. The problem with this little tiny word is that it's one of the first words we learn when we come into the world. We are taught to say hello, goodbye, Mummy, Daddy, please, thank you, yes and *no*. And the one we say the most is *no, no, no!*

▶ We didn't want to go to bed.

▶ We didn't want to eat our greens.

▶ We didn't want to wash behind our ears.

▶ We didn't want to go to school.

▶ We didn't want to clean our shoes.

▶ We didn't want to clean our rooms.

So as we've grown up, naturally it's become a word we are not overly keen on. No wonder we do everything in our power to stay well away from it! We quickly say 'Yes', just to get away from that word!

Our brains are so clever, they store everything; even if you don't think of something, your brain has it stored away in the subconscious. So all the times you've been told 'No' are stored in your mind. I wouldn't mind guessing that you have more happy memories attached to the word 'Yes' than to the 'No's. So it's not surprising that we often don't appreciate how this natural fear is eating away at your chance of success.

Let's start by looking at the 'can you just-ers'. They seem harmless, right? And they tend to be really nice people, because 'can you just-ers' tend to be good with people and know how to make things happen. And while you are helping them out, they are able to get on with what they want to achieve. Remember in Chapter 5, we talked about how to achieve success you need to ask for help? Well, the 'can you just-ers' have no issue asking for help! They know that, while you do their dogsbody work, they can be getting on with looking awesome and rocketing their success, keeping their goals on track. And as this happens over time you will start to feel resentful. You start to recognise why they are phoning or walking towards you with a smile on their face – because you know what's coming next! The 'can you just-ers' always smile and thank you; however, a smile and a thank you is not going to take you up the career ladder is it? A 'No' just might.

However, you don't need to say the actual word.

E – Examples and exercises

Example

One gentleman I worked with was employed in a large department where no one answered their phones. Why? Because they knew this gentleman was so conscientious that he would do anything to make the company look good. Why bother answering your phone if that guy will do it? We can get on with the real work and ignore our phones. And he ended up looking like he was slacking. He missed deadlines and targets. And when we worked together, he showed he had a massive fear of ignoring the phones, in case it impacted on the company.

Yes, he was conscientious; however, when we raised his awareness of what he was agreeing to, of how badly he was respected in the department and how little chance he had of promotion compared to his work colleagues, suddenly the phones looked like public enemy number one!

We worked out how to reframe his view of the phones and, I'm happy to say, the gentleman in question now has a team of 40+! When you say 'Yes' all the time that is the damage you too could be creating to your own success.

Exercise 1 – Can you just-er strategies

"Lack of planning on your part does not constitute an emergency on mine."

So, let's look at the tools and techniques you'll need to say 'No' in the nicest possible way. Before I help you create a strategy to deal with the 'can you just-ers', I want to share with you a beautiful quote from a business friend's husband. David Pattrick, who unfortunately is no longer with us, always said: 'Lack of planning on your part does not constitute an emergency on mine'. It's good to remember this silently in your head when dealing with 'can you just-ers', for a number of reasons.

1 By constantly helping the 'can you just-ers' you are taking away their opportunity to learn new skills, and their ability to prioritise and to organise. Do they need to learn these skills? Is it a case that they aren't very good at these tasks or don't enjoy them, or just see you as someone that is an easy target or better at it than them? (whichever it is, knowing this will be important for your strategy).

2 If you are constantly helping a 'can you just-er', then how is anyone going to know that person's weaknesses? How will they know that this person needs support to grow? Are there other people that need assistance like this within the company? Perhaps there are those that lack the communication skills that a 'can you just-er' has to get the job done and so are quietly struggling. This could mean that the organisation is missing out on an opportunity to improve profitability and productivity because you are, in effect hiding, an issue that is impacting on the company as a whole.

3 If you are being made to feel uncomfortable and put-upon, isn't it likely other people are too? Strong-willed people have a habit of getting what they want because they can use communication powerfully (especially the word 'No'). Learning these tools will help you learn new

strategies to help you be a powerful communicator and a strong-willed person that can say 'No' too.

Knowing this information means that you are able to work out a strategy to deal with these people in a way that creates win–win relationships. I feel it is very important when creating success that you create relationships that enable both parties to walk away feeling they got a fair deal, a 50/50 split (it's good for you and your success in other ways too, which we will cover in a later chapter).

"It is very important when creating success that you create relationships that enable both parties to walk away feeling they got a fair deal, a 50/50 split. "

Professional relationships need to be a two-way street with both parties benefiting and delivering, instead of you just give, give giving. We will talk more about win–win relationships in Chapter 8 but, needless to say, they are a critical component to winning at work.

This is the case of the 'can you just-ers' who you struggle to say 'No' to. You understand the impact that always saying 'Yes' can have on your success. Now it's time to work out how to say 'No' to them in a way that is respectful and gets you the result you want.

Think about the person that always asks for a small favour. A quick job that will only take you a couple of minutes. What are the ways you could handle it? Firstly, consider the kind of person you are: if you are a shy and quiet person, it is no good suggesting that you just tell them to go away. First, that would be rude. Second, it would be unlikely to win you any friends on the road to success (and, as we learnt in Chapter 5, success needs the right support.) Third, it would take you so far out of your comfort zone it would never happen!

So what would work for you? What is your natural style? How do you deal with difficult situations? Some people always say 'Yes', because it's easier. However, is it really easy? By always saying 'Yes', what are you agreeing to?

Let's learn some strategies to help you feel confident about saying 'No' (without having to say the word 'No'.)

You may find that for the first time you still end up doing the 'favour', however, even if you don't get the result you want. That is still a success, because you had a go at saying 'No'. Each time you will get better at it. Ask yourself questions like:

▶ What did I do?

▶ What do I feel worked?

▶ Where do I feel I could improve?

▶ What do I feel could have worked better?

▶ What question could I have asked them that would have put the responsibility back on them?

▶ What would have made me feel more confident?

Each time we try, failure is not a fail unless we never have another go. So practise, practise, practise.

Let's look at some phrases to use, and how you could make them work for you. Remember, they've got to feel natural to you:

▶ **'I too struggled with this** – perhaps another time I can sit down and work through a few of these with you so you can get the hang of it. I too have a deadline of 5 pm.'

▶ **'I would have loved to help** – however, I have a deadline of 5 pm. Next time, just give me a call in the morning and we can work on this together. We would need to clear about 45 minutes.'

▶ **'You know I used to hate these too** – but I found by doing a, b and c I can now clear these in less than an hour. Would you like me to teach you?'

▶ **'I've a meeting with so and so next week** – shall we discuss it with them then and get you some support to learn this system better?'

▶ **'Everything you need is already on this page of the website** – because this comes up a lot. Anything you can't find, just let me know and together we can plan a time to rewrite it. Does that sound good?'

▶ **'I'm happy to do this for you on this occasion** – what I will do is copy in our manager so they are aware that this is proving an issue for us both and impacting on our work.'

Notice none of these examples use the word 'No'? Notice how they all give the ownership of the work back to the 'can you just-er'? Notice how you are offering to be of assistance, while making it clear that you are just as busy as them with your own career and success plans? You are both equally important, right? Notice how you are returning the conversation back to them, like lobbing a ball over the net in tennis, it is now their responsibility to do something with it, not yours.

Exercise 2 – The power of words

Remember not to use words that place blame. It's all too easy to be thinking things like:

▶ 'Lazy! They always ask me to do this!'

▶ 'I knew they shouldn't have been standing around drinking coffee!'

▶ 'I'm not staying late so they can go down the pub again, it's their problem!'

▶ 'I'm fed up with making you look good and you earn more than me and never tell the boss I helped you!'

So keep your thoughts in check. And in that way your negative language is not likely to slip into the conversation. Creating blame risks raising their hackles and they may try to pull rank or make you feel guilty. It is also good to not ask questions that start with 'Why?'; far better to start with questions that start with 'What', because 'what' questions are less likely to create guilt. Try it for yourself:|

▶ 'Why did you do that?'

▶ 'What are the reasons you did that?'

▶ 'Why will you not be able to help?'

▶ 'What are the reasons you won't be able to help?'

▶ 'Why didn't you get this done yesterday?'

▶ 'What are the reasons this has been left until today?'

See how questions like this constantly help shift the responsibility and ownership of the issue back to the 'can you just-ers'? Questions can be really powerful and can create the space to let the other party take ownership of what is going on. I know this because I've coached many people and helped them do just that! Aim to keep the negativity out of the conversation and there will be very little reason to use the word 'No'.

Exercise 3 – Repercussions game

Let's play the repercussions game shall we? Let's play the 'What if?' game to destruction. Remember, by exposing a fear for how silly and unlikely it is, we are able to start to bring it back to a realistic and manageable place. You are far more likely to be able to deal with a fear if it *feels* smaller. Fears are allowed to grow in size and gain big scary teeth dripping with venom when you allow them to infect your mind. So, instead of allowing a fear to grow, let's start chipping away at it and bringing it down to size, shall we?

▶ What if I say 'No' and the boss sacks me?

▶ What if I say 'No' and they tell everyone in the country I'm too stupid to do it?

▶ What if I say 'No' and my work colleague punches me?

▶ What if I say 'No' and they cry?

▶ What if I say 'No' and throw everything on my desk on the floor?

▶ What if I say 'No' and they throw themselves on the floor and throw a tantrum like a toddler, screaming that I'm a big fat meany head?

"*Remember, by exposing a fear for how silly and unlikely it is, we are able to start to bring it back to a realistic and manageable place.*"

How far-fetched can you make your questions? Another reason we are fearful of saying 'No' is because we may worry about what people may think of us. You've got to look like a team player, right? You've got to look capable of everything, right? However, when you are asked to do anything and everything ask yourself, 'Does this fit into my goals?', 'Does this fit into my success plans?'

Ask yourself 'Who sets my goals?' Are you working with someone to achieve them? And, if so, what do they say? Have you asked them what their viewpoint is?

Exercise 4 – Your natural style

This is a great exercise to remember for other fears as well as the fear of saying 'No'. I want you to think of somewhere that you are comfortable – not your sofa on a Sunday night; I mean in your professional career. Somewhere you feel you naturally shine, where things seem to flow. Somewhere where know you are good and you can achieve. What do you notice? Maybe it is in the office at your desk where you can easily multitask? What do you do well – naturally? And don't tell me you don't. Because *everyone* does something really well. You may have to really listen to yourself, think hard and delve a bit deeper than usual. You may have to stop being dismissive of your talents. I know you can come up with a place where you naturally feel like you fit perfectly and perform brilliantly. It doesn't matter where it is. What matters is what you notice:

▶ Is it the way you are feeling?

▶ Is it what you can see?

▶ Is it what you are doing?

- Is it what you can hear?
- Are you alone?
- Do you need equipment?
- Are you in an office or in front of a laptop, do you have a pen in hand?

Really notice it in your own way. For some this is easy. They can visualise it and see every aspect of it as if they were there. If that's not you, flick through your diary and look at what you've been doing over the last few months, at what stands out as a great day that just flowed with ease. Why was that?

By doing this exercise you will be able to understand more about the kind of person you are. By knowing more about the person you are, what matters to you, what you like and what your natural style is, you will be able to replicate these skills again and again.

Now list the things you noticed, whether you choose to physically write them down or list them in your head. And by working *with* yourself, and not *against*, your natural style you will be able to power up your results. This list could say (but is not restricted to):

- I was happy.
- I was relaxed.
- I was organised.
- The phone was turned off.
- I was alone.
- I had written a list.
- I had gone to bed early the night before.
- I had just received good news.
- I was the first person in the office.

What made it onto your list? Now, before you work out your strategy for saying 'No', write out this list. Print it and put it in your diary, on your desk, or on your screen saver. Maybe frame it or put it in a fridge magnet on your fridge. I don't mind where you put it, but it needs to be your visual reminder that this is your natural style for winning at work. This is your way of making things happen. Here is an example for you. You like (for instance) to be in the office early, in a quiet office, away from the chatty people, with a list of work for the day, knowing that you've already cleared the important work that had to be in for Mrs Smith even though the deadline is Friday (because otherwise it plays on your mind), and that way you have brain space to concentrate on new things.

If you want to achieve more, knowing your natural style can really help. So please take a few moments to do this; your professional success could profit immensely. Sometimes we surprise ourselves. For instance, writing this book I learnt I like a pot of tea. It takes discipline to write a book and I've not experienced a pot of tea since my Nan used to berate me that my tea was so weak it was a fortnight!

> **"If you want to achieve more, knowing your natural style can really help."**

Knowing your natural style could really help you understand where you feel more confident and comfortable to say 'It is unacceptable that you are choosing to manipulate my time and my working success in this way'. Exciting isn't it?

A – Actions

I think the most powerful reason to change the amount of time you say 'Yes' to everyone is to ask yourself this question every time someone asks you if you can do something for them. And it is this: 'If you keep saying "Yes" to everyone, what are you agreeing to?'

How does everyone else's 'Yes' impact on your success? This is not about 'working within acceptable parameters'. This is about talking to the right people to find out how you create a better way of working. Raise awareness to the right people that this is happening and is there a better way that we can do this?

Maybe you have a better way in mind? In which case this could be your chance to really shine and step above the precipice and get seen for all the right reasons. Yes, that could be scary, but it could also be your chance to shine and really win at work! Do you feel you know the solution? Could your solution increase productivity for the company and not just yourself and your colleagues?

Act it!

Another way to deal with the fear of saying 'No' is to look at who is really good at saying 'No'. Now here is a saying you don't expect to hear from me, however I will say it anyway: I've always admired politicians for their ability to say 'No'.

They can skirt around that word 'No' like a prima ballerina and wrap you in words so sweetly you can't even remember the question that was first asked. Okay so we've become far more savvy to that; however, just listen to a politician say 'No'.

Who do you know that says 'No' to something in such a way that everyone walks away feeling like they got the result they wanted and yet it was actually only one person that got what they wanted?

▶ What attributes do they have?

▶ How do they talk?

▶ How do they stand?

▶ How do they speak? Do they speak fast or slow? Do they have a high voice or a low one?

▶ How do they make people feel?

Find people that you admire for their ability to communicate in a way that makes everyone feel special and they still get the results they want. By observing other people that are experts at getting on with their own work, and keeping focused on their own goals you will find ways to stay dedicated to your own goals to ensure you have the ability to say 'No' when needed.

R – Results

Ultimately everyone is responsible for their own success. By learning to say 'No' you are helping others to take responsibility for their own success. You are also not preventing other people from learning new skills to succeed and rocket their own success!

Lastly on this subject if you want to master the skill of saying 'No'. Then master the skill of thinking yes. If you are deciding to say 'No' to things because they leave you overburdened, moving away from your own goals and success, consider these questions:

▶ What would you like to say 'Yes' to?

▶ What are the opportunities you would like?

▶ Who in the office would you love to ask for your help?

▶ Who would you happily give an hour of your time to, so that you could showcase how good you could be for their business and success?

▶ Who would you love to work with?

"Ultimately everyone is responsible for their own success. By learning to say 'No' you are helping others to take responsibility for their own success."

Remember if you don't power up your thoughts with what you want to achieve, your brain will naturally revert into a more negative stage. Our brains are a muscle and as with all muscles, if you don't use them you lose them. So power up your thoughts when it comes to saying 'No' to the things that stand in the way of your success and know what you would love to say 'Yes' to.

7

I'm petrified of public speaking

As you may be learning with this book, not all fears make themselves brutally known. Some hide in our minds and attack our success, thus they have to be found to be dealt with, almost snipered out of existence. Anyone I've ever worked with a fear of public speaking will tell me that this is not the case with a fear of public speaking. A fear of public speaking is not subtle. It does not hide its intentions.

F – The fear

A fear of public speaking can at the least make you nervous and feel like you are going to forget what you want to say and at its worse physically close up your throat, make you sweat, your hands shake. Your heart can feel like it's pounding so hard it's going to come out of your chest. And you feel like the pressure in your head means your head is going to explode too. I speak here not just from years of helping people with their fear of public speaking, I speak from my own fear of it too.

Years ago I had such a fear of public speaking the first time I was asked to speak at a professional development day for business owners for 20 minutes that I was literally in the rest rooms wishing I could collapse and receive medical assistance. I knew that to be successful I had to overcome the fear, and somehow someone that sounded like me said 'Yes, I would love to speak at your big event in front of 50+ people', and yet inside I was praying my spleen would explode and I could escape this conversation, take down my website and online marketing and hide in Bolivia for the rest of my life.

So I know what that fear is like. I also know how to fix it. You could still be questioning why you need to bother fixing this fear. I worked with one business woman who had successfully manoeuvred herself out of speaking engagements for 20 years. However, as we looked at this fear, she realised the impact that it had had on her career could have been catastrophic. Public speaking is not all standing in front of 50 people or in a room the size of stadium and getting a message across that makes the audience cheer and cry out 'You rock!' Sometimes public speaking is about being able to get your message across in a small group of possibly only four or five people but being able to successfully control the group so that you are not spoken over, dismissed and made to feel like your opinion didn't matter.

❝Sometimes public speaking is about being able to get your message across in a small group of possibly only four or five people.❞

Have any of these happened to you?

▶ Have you ever been in a group environment and felt like what you had to say didn't get heard?

▶ Have you left a conversation and thought, 'I wish I had said that!'

▶ Have you got tongue tied and sat down thinking, 'What did I say!'

▶ Have you looked at other people in the room and thought, 'I wish you would shut up for a minute and let me talk!'

▶ Have you thought, 'I know what I want to say it's just I can't say that to you!'

If any of these have ever happened to you, or you have your own thoughts on speaking up, then this chapter is going to help you overcome the fear of speaking anywhere, for any occasion. It's a powerful point to remember that this could overspill into every aspect of your life. Want a new car and are nervous of telling the sales man what you really want and not what they want to sell you? Want to get your family to listen to what you have to say? Want to get heard at the school PTA? I once read that the skill of effective communication was by far the most powerful impactor on your success. And I would agree. The case study in this chapter had a massive impact on this woman's career from the moment she dealt with it. And she had put up with the fear for 20 years!

This fear can manifest itself in so many ways. You can end up looking like the person that always says 'No' to the speaking slot at networking. Or the chance to present at work. 'Don't ask them, they won't do it.' What's that doing to your career? To your success? Does that make you look like a team player? Someone that can be relied on? Someone that can rise to any challenge? If someone is scared of presenting to 10 colleagues, can we trust that person to deal with our biggest clients? To bring in the big contracts? Are you bringing in an element of doubt on your abilities to those around you because you won't do it? Or don't do it with style and confidence?

Take a moment to ask yourself if you do shy away from speaking up and presenting. And ask yourself what impact is it having on your success. Sometimes public speaking is just about having the confidence to say your own opinion. In this chapter we will look at the physical, the emotional and the physiological things you can do to be able to successfully public speak in any environment.

"Sometimes public speaking is just about having the confidence to say your own opinion."

E – Examples and exercises

Example

This business woman who I briefly mentioned above had swerved and dived out of the way of every speaking engagement for 20 years. And now she was faced with a speaking engagement she could not pass to a member of staff. They really, really wanted just her. This woman was incredibly talented, professional and exceptionally well respected in her profession and had managed to hide her public speaking fear for years.

This time it was not a speaking engagement for 50 people at work. This was at a national conference introducing a piece of work, on a stage with a microphone. As a first-time speaker, this was hardly a gentle introduction to public speaking. The absolute terror it created in her meant that she had to deal with it. She saw it as an imovable obstacle in the way of her success and so she called me.

We worked together to understand why public speaking was a fear of hers. How can someone so well respected within her industry fear standing up and introducing something? She had been asked to do this. They wanted her. By looking at the fact that of the 300 people in the room they wanted just her, she was able to see that she was in fact 'their expert of choice'. We worked on building her self-confidence by considering the fact that, although she was in a room full of her peers, they weren't as she believed looking down their noses at her. They weren't waiting for her to fail. (Yes we played the 'What if?' game!) They wanted to hear what she had to say. She was their expert of choice. And the biggest lesson she learnt was that she had to accept that she was an expert. That 300 people respected her as one. We worked physically, emotionally and psychologically on this.

Okay so yes it was still scary. The thing with fear is it doesn't go just because you ask it to. We created the tools and techniques to get her through the speaking engagement. And I also suggested she text me just before she went on. I texted her back reminding her how awesome she was. Not my opinion I hasten to add, but that of the 300 people in her audience. And she did it. One of the physical things we created for her was that she felt very comfortable on the telephone, so we practised in our session imagining that the microphone was in fact a telephone. Using visual clues can really help when you want to achieve something new, especially when fear is playing a big part in your head. Visual clues can help override the brain's natural response.

"The thing with fear is it doesn't go just because you ask it to."

Within an hour of that business woman being on stage doing something she has shied away from for 20 years, I got a text to say, 'Not only did I do it, I've agreed to speak at two other engagements!' Now just think what that could do for her career!

When it comes to your own fear of public speaking, if you've explored how it manifests itself, how does it make you feel? Really explore that feeling. How bad is it? If you could quantify it what would that look like? How would you describe it?

Exercise 1 – The 'What if?' game

Use the negative spiral to really understand the impact the public speaking fear has on your success. What actions does it stop you from taking?

▶ What effect does that have on you personally and professionally?

▶ What does that mean you tell yourself or think about yourself?

What's the best outcomes I could imagine? (Regardless of time, money or skill restraints)	What's the worst outcomes I could imagine? (Think silly and far-fetched here – let your mind go crazy, remember the 'You lose, your home, job and live in a cave off of mud and rain water all because you asked for what you want' 'What if' game in Chapter 2? That silly!)

Now it's a good idea to play the 'What if?' game, in two ways:

By doing this you are able to start challenging your natural style of thinking and that means your mind opens up to a new way of thinking. Great, right? Just remember, if our case study can change a way of thinking that was heavily ingrained for 20 years in one session, you can in a chapter.

A – Actions

I read a great piece of research by Dana Carney, Amy Cuddy and Andy Yap that said that if you stood like a superhero you could physically change the way you acted. And you could change your success rate. Stand with your feet shoulder-width apart, shoulders back, think all Wonder Woman or Batman (there's enough of them to choose one you like) as if you've kicked the baddies' butt and saved the world from destruction and not one hair is out of place; okay, so there's a neat smudge on your right cheek. But hey all in a day's work for a superhero, right? Chest out, head up, proud, confident and capable of anything. And it was said that if you stood like that you could in fact be more successful. Perform better, get better results. As with so many great studies within the year a study came along that disproved the first study. And then others went on to prove it was true again. Whether the study is true or not there is a lot to be said about the way something makes us feel.

Try it for a moment. Wherever you are right now, round your shoulders and tilt forward. Frown. And look down. Pull your chin down to your chest and don't make eye contact. Breathe in short breaths and imagine how that would feel if you were presenting. Now sit up right. Shoulders back. Head back. Smile. Make eye contact, chest up, look up, deep breath and imagine how that would feel if you were about to speak publicly. Take it one step further and imagine if you added to the equation the way you were feeling.

❝Chest out, head up, proud, confident and capable of anything.❞

Try it:

▶ Do the negative pose and think negatively and see how that feels.

▶ Then do the negative pose and think positively.

▶ Now do the positive pose and think negatively.

▶ Finally do the positive pose and think positively.

Can you see some of the actions you need to take? You need to stand with purpose not with a porpoise (again, that's where the slide of me and the porpoise comes out because it makes you laugh and takes away a second of the fear that public speaking creates).

What *feels* like a good way to stand to you? Before we look at the words or the emotional and psychological things we can do to help you feel confident in dealing with this fear you need to learn to stand in a way that says 'I'm ready for action'. You will need to practise this.

A really good way to do this is to stand in front of a mirror. It's really unnerving and it's completely unnatural to talk to yourself in the mirror; however, if you can talk to yourself in the mirror, an audience will be a bit easier. Won't it? So practise standing in front of the mirror and striking different poses. What makes you feel comfortable?

A lot of people worry about what to do with their hands. Politicians get hours of coaching on how to ensure they keep their palms up (so they look open and honest) rather than forcing their hands down (and are forcing their opinions upon you) so if you find your hands become out of control let them clasp together naturally. When I was a bridesmaid many years ago the photographer said that the bouquet should end up lowered half way down our legs so that the middle of our arm was over our hip. If you do this, pose with your hands naturally clasped not gripped together. Then you will be able to still move your hands around, although the movement will be subtler and controlled.

Should I stand still or move around? To answer this, it's a good idea to think 'Who am I talking to?' Is your audience expecting a fast-paced talk? A professional talk? A relaxed conversation? An in-depth monologue? A discussion? By thinking about the expectations of your audience you can start to consider what kind of behaviour you think they are going to expect from you.

"By thinking about the expectations of your audience, you can start to consider what kind of behaviour you think they are going to expect from you."

If you are talking to a room full of people that want to be motivated and inspired, then it's fine to be someone that moves around the room. On the other hand, if you want to appear professional and gain the attention of your audience, maybe giving your audience brain ache by trying to keep up with your athletics is not the best idea. So work out a natural balance between standing still and movement. Movement also stops your audience becoming bored. Remember, with the greatest will in the world, the greatest orators still know that an audience has a limited attention span.

The important point to remember in the actions point of this chapter is that to override and eradicate this fear you need to learn new skills. You need to learn new techniques. Not all fears will be overridden with just a belief. To really banish them for good, you need to learn new skills to accompany your mindset. Here I'm sharing a few tools and physical techniques. However, there are far more learned authors out there than myself to share ideas on how to be an expert speaker. The greatest book I read was given to me by a great speaker, Colin McLean (I will share his top piece of advice in a moment). He has worked with the BBC and many aspiring great business leaders and TV presenters to help them become great public speakers. The book in question is called *Lend Me Your Ears* by Max Atkinson, well worth a read on how to be a first-class public speaker.

Colin beautifully summed up public speaking for me. Take into account that I had experienced a tremendous fear of public speaking, so to speak before a great such as Colin McLean (and know he was in my audience) brought many a fear back. To then be handed a copy of Max Atkinson's book by said Colin drooped my shoulders and made me feel like a chastised little girl who's just been told 'must do better'.

In his perfect-tone voice Colin said, 'On the contrary Mandie you are someone that can appreciate the true meaning to find your own style and be proud of it.' He was right. Above all else a few years earlier, when Colin had first heard me speak I had cornered him afterwards and, being someone always keen to learn and grow, had been desperate to learn from such a great man. 'How can I improve, Colin?' 'What did I do wrong?' I'd begged to know. And his reply had infuriated me: 'Nothing, it was perfect. Beautifully matched to your passion and enthusiasm and motivation for business and success of others.' As I recall I had been quite disgruntled at the time at this response; however, now I can appreciate that what Colin was saying is very true. If you have a fear of public speaking style, you will know you have overcome that hurdle and massive obstacle in the road to your success when you have a natural style that you don't constantly second guess. Yes, you will always be looking to improve, add new content, learn new techniques, trial new ideas. However, you will trust that you are capable and have a style that is all your own.

> **"If you have a fear of public speaking style, you will know you have overcome that hurdle and massive obstacle in the road to your success when you have a natural style that you don't constantly second guess."**

Here are a few more tools to add to your actions to override that public speaking fear:

▶ **Practise – a lot!** And don't just practise from the start. I once saw a man stand on a stage with impeccable notes only to drop said notes and then spend the first 5 minutes apologising for the dropped notes! Practise from the middle to the end and then the start. Practise from the end to the middle. In this way, if you get heckled (read on for a few top tips on hecklers or 'I need to prove I'm as clever as you's') you are okay to pick up from where you left off. And you will feel comfortable to do so. Don't feel rigid in what you are saying (unless that is what is asked of the speaking engagement); most speaking engagements like fluidity.

▶ **But don't practise too much.** I hear the saying practise, practise, practise; however, if you have a fear of public speaking, you can work yourself back into the fear! As you practise, remember the other elements of this chapter: the tools that are powering up your mindset. If you are a visual person and are going to rely on visual aids, then rehearse with these too. However, over-rehearsing will be like that moment before an exam when you end up standing with the person who seems to have crammed and studied far harder than anyone else and makes you panic that you've not done enough. And *that* you don't need.

▶ **Don't read from notes.** You are an expert in your field. You've been asked to speak because of that. It's something I always repeat to someone with a fear of public speaking. A photographer is not asked to speak on the intricacies of brain surgeries to a room full of brain surgeons. One of the reasons we feel fear when public speaking is because we fear what people are thinking. (It's such a big issue it has its own chapter!) However, for now, just remember you've been asked to speak because you *know* what you are talking about. People aren't trying to catch you out. So please remember this: People actually *want* to hear what you have to say. They start on your side. The poor guy who dropped his notes. There he was on stage feeling awful. And what he didn't understand or couldn't appreciate because he was too mortified was we were all feeling for him and rooting for him to do well. So much so that I went up and told him so afterwards! However, when you read from notes you take away a little of your professionalism. Try it. Stand in front of a mirror and deliver your speech with and without paper. You will note your delivery changes. The way you stand. What you do with your hands. Even the way you breathe. So please get rid of the paper. The only time you want to read from paper is if you want to reinforce something. For example, it's not just me saying this, 'Here is Dr Jones' opinion on this too' or if you are sharing a testimonial that someone has given of you.

▶ **Remember you've every right to be in that room.** You are the expert of choice. In Chapter 10 we will get your mind under control on what you should be thinking; for now, just accept that it is as important as the skills you learn, the way you stand.

► **Don't apologise if you get something wrong.** Remember only you know what you were going to say. I've been at events when the speaker has veered so far off of the title of the talk and yet the audience has still loved it!

► **Unless you need to, don't use jargon.** Jargon risks alienating your audience. It's used by people who want to look clever. It's only really expected in certain arenas and you will know which ones they are. Which leads me on to hecklers.

Hecklers may ask clever questions or awkward questions. I've had ones who are annoyed it's not them on stage. I've had ones that are annoyed that the government have cut their funds and they've got to listen to this woman tell them how to grow their business. When you have to present in a hostile environment, remember it's not your fault. That is their agenda, not yours. You were asked to speak, they weren't. Still their problem: still not yours. You are still awesome. If anything, as scary as that is, it means you are the organisers' expert of choice. And remember from Chapter 4, there is a fine line between arrogance and confidence, so accept a quiet inner confidence that says 'I'm the expert they chose'. With that in mind, you still have the person with their nose out of joint to deal with. Getting embroiled in a debate is not fair on the rest of your audience and not professional. At all times you want to ask yourself, 'What is the result I want from this speaking engagement?' It is highly likely you want to walk away looking professional and someone that can be relied on, right? So with that in mind here are some great things to say, and yes a couple I've actually used to great effect (and created great opportunities – so I know they work!):

> **"When you have to present in a hostile environment, remember it's not your fault. That is their agenda, not yours."**

► That is a good point. I've got five minutes at the end, so let's explore that more when we have the time as we need to cover a lot in the next half hour.

► I really appreciate you highlighting that point. That is similar to the issue that so many clients are experiencing, so if you would like to take a seat I can show you how we've worked to solve it for them and you can tell me at the end if you feel these ideas would work for you on a no-money, no-time budget.

► I knew I would get one person in the room that would disagree, tell me why you feel you are more like a striped hog-nosed skunk than a human. (That person turned into a client the same day!)

► That is a great question, I will need to look into that for you. May I get your card so that I can?

► You raise a good point. However, it's important we explain why you do this, before we explain how to, and thank you for bringing this to the room so early in the day's training. (Ideal for the disgruntled person that feels they should be delivering the training and want to point out they know as much as you and want every opportunity to prove it!)

Aim not to use words like 'Try', and 'But', or questions that start with 'Why'. For instance:

| Let's try to do this shall we? | Becomes | Let's aim to prove this shall we? |

(Try is wishy-washy, you want to reinforce your professionalism and confidence.)

| Why are you doing it like that? | Becomes | What are the reasons that you are doing it like that? |

('Why' sentences add blame and in a group environment. You don't want to add blame, you want to enable the opportunity to explore and get results. And by being the nice person, that means that you will be liked for your style of presenting too!)

The final action that you need to remember, is to remember to breathe. I know that sounds daft, but if you listen to yourself as a scared public speaker, you will realise that you don't breathe a great deal. Hence the short breath, heart racing and light headedness. Put your hand on your stomach and practise making your hand go up and down. If you are breathing from your chest, then you are breathing too shallowly and causing yourself stress. Also allow yourself a few . . . pauses . . . pauses are good for two reasons.

Firstly, they allow you to breathe. And secondly, they enable you to add emphasis to certain words within your presentation. They also enable your audience to think about what you have said. Then trial it to see where you should add a pause. And when I've run master classes on this, and have asked people to put long pauses in their presentations. A few seconds can feel like a lifetime, but it's a really nice opportunity for your audience to process information and reflect. And seconds are not as long as you think, so try it and see. The traditional 60-second elevator pitch is a good example of this. In 60 seconds you can say so much and yet a few great pauses can be just as powerful within those precious 60 seconds. If you network, it's a great opportunity to overcome your public speaking fear and trial the actions and exercise within this chapter until you find your natural style.

" A few seconds can feel like a lifetime, but it's a really nice opportunity for your audience to process information and reflect. "

R – Results

And the reason you need to trial the tools and strategies in this chapter is because we want to see this fear obliterated. So that no matter what comes up in your professional life, you are not looking over your shoulder worrying about the time someone says, 'You can do a presentation on that right?'

As we've seen, some fears are sneaky and some fears are in your face. Some fears are fixed with a thought and some need a bit of work. I would say that to fix this fear, start with a belief that you can fix it and you will. Then move on to looking at the skills and tools that will reinforce it for you, and is completed with practice and action. This fear is shrunk to a non-entity by doing it again and again so that you feel your confidence grow. Don't make the assumption that every time will be perfect. However, do make the assumption that every time you are growing and learning from the experience and improving your performance.

I can give you so many wonderful examples of the results here: The business woman who told me that I would 'never get her speaking to 50 business owners' who within a short time texted me to say 'I've just spoke to a room full of business owners *with* a microphone *and* I got new business out of it!'; The business owner who practised what they would say and how they would say it and gained a dream contract. One they wouldn't have dreamed of going for because, well, it involved a table of people in front of them and that business owner doing all the talking. What would they say?

Remember, to get results in public speaking there is an element of skill. I think the story that will stick with me always on the need for an element of skill is dear MacArthur Wheeler. And I share this short, funny but true, story in the hope it will also stick with you to empower your success too.

"*Remember, to get results in public speaking there is an element of skill.*"

MacArthur Wheeler read that lemon juice could be used to help you write secret letters. If you wrote with lemon juice it couldn't be seen unless you had a UV light. He reasoned that if that was true, then if he smeared lemon juice over his face then he would be unable to be seen. And if he couldn't be seen then he could successfully rob his local bank. And like any sensible bank robber he decided to test his theory by taking a selfie. Unfortunately, being the mid-90s alas there was not a great deal of technology around so he used his trusted polaroid camera that enabled him to take an instant picture. However, the film in the camera was damaged and his image didn't come out. Thus MacArthur reasoned he was invisible. MacArthur robbed two banks in one day. When he was arrested later that night he retorted, 'But I wore the juice!'

So remember, don't be a MacArthur Wheeler if you want to be successful in public speaking, if you want to eradicate that fear, you won't do it just by reading this chapter and 'winging it'.

Remember, by not taking action what are you agreeing to? Think back to the negative spiral and the impact that this has on your success at work and how it could potentially manifest further, therefore effecting your future success Is that enough to make you take action on this?

I hate phoning people

F – Fear

There are over 6.8 billion phones in the world so how can phoning people be a fear? And yet when I work with people on their success it never ceases to amaze me that when you discuss people's plan of action, their way to achieve ultimate success, their way to get results, to get the deal signed they are going to send an email. An email!

Not arrange a meeting. Not pick up the phone and talk to them. Not pop in and see them. I know we live in a fast-paced world where everyone wants everything yesterday. I know we live in a world where we want proof we did our bit of the job, so here's a paper trail as long as a marathon, but seriously, an email? You trust an email to deliver your success?

"You trust an email to deliver your success?"

Communication for success is a little like fashion. It goes around and around (flares apparently are back in fashion every 10 years!). Years ago if you wanted success you would write a letter. Then everyone realised that this was a good idea, and businesses were set up that would write the letters for you and the next thing you know your door mat was covered in not letters but junk mail. Years later the world wide web was invented. And word processors turned into computers. We could talk to people anywhere, and so we did. Suddenly we could keep people updated on anything. We could look ultra-efficient and organised and show we cared with an email. But hang on, now there's a plethora of companies that will write emails for you and our inboxes are full of not emails but junk mail, accept we don't call it junk mail we call it spam. Are you still trusting email to deliver your success?

It scares me how many people send one email and expect it to get to the person they want it to and it will magically get answered above everything else that has appeared in their inbox as well as everything else that has appeared on that person's desk and in their diary. And yet you don't use that phone you have welded to your side, for what reason?

- ▶ You don't know what to say?
- ▶ What if you say the wrong thing?
- ▶ What if they are busy?
- ▶ What if you annoy them?
- ▶ What if they don't want what you're offering?

The list is quite extensive as to why you shouldn't ring them, right? And so you don't, you hide behind email. Because let's be honest if you don't actually pick up the phone then you don't actually know and it's like you are delaying the inevitable. You can lie to yourself that you aren't going to get fired or lose this opportunity. If you don't pick the phone, in your mind there is a parallel universe where it might just have worked out.

It's the scourge of the 21st-century communications success. And it becomes a fear to pick up the phone and it could be seriously publicly damaging your success. I've been at a networking event and I've shivered in horror to overhear a conversation where people seem in love with each other's companies and they finish the conversation with 'I will email you to arrange a date to meet up'. Sorry! What? You will *email* to arrange a date? What's wrong with arranging it *now* while we are in the same room? Its mind-blowingly annoying!! (I would add far more exclamation marks; however, I fear my publishers will remove them all.)

The fact is that it's becoming increasing obvious to me that communication needs to be taught in schools because if you want to succeed, communication skills are still the biggest requirement of your life. And yet they are not taught as a lesson. Do you understand the difference between one type of sigh over the phone and another? I do, but then that's because I'm fascinated by non-verbal communication (and it means when someone thinks they are hiding their true emotions and feelings on a subject they actually are still giving me clues!) You too could be picking up on these, if you picked up the phone. People think that on the phone they can hide their emotions; however, it doesn't take a lot of practice to be able to pick up on the subtle clues that are given away by people on the phone and that could seriously power up your phone call success. And that could make you feel a lot more confident and that in turn could really kick the fear's butt!

> **"If you want to succeed, communication skills are still the biggest requirement of your life."**

I've even had people email me to want to arrange a time to phone me so that we can arrange to skype. So while you're still laughing at the absurdness of that, ask yourself if you pick up the phone and ask for what you want and not phone people shouting, 'Show me the money!' I mean phone people to:

▶ Ask confidently for that meeting to discuss how your company can help them.

▶ Ask why did you not reply to our email regarding the contract.

▶ Ask why did I not get the job; could I get some feedback please.

▶ Ask for five minutes to look at the reasons why it's a 'No', so you can learn from them and get a 'Yes'.

▶ Ask for a testimonial and one other person who would love what we do please.

▶ Ask for the opportunity to discuss if you could explore how we could work together because you feel you have something you could offer.

All of the above are scary beyond words. I completely understand that. And all of the above I've assisted people to do. However, if you don't deal with the fear of picking up the phone and asking your own questions and dealing with your own fear, what are you agreeing to? What impact is it having on your success?

E – Examples and exercises

Example

When I've asked people why they hide behind email quite often the reply is: 'But people like you are really busy'. Here's an example of the reply:

Me: 'You are right, I am, which means I don't get long in the office to answer emails, so what do you think that means for you?

Phone fearer: 'That you get a lot of email and could have missed mine.'

Me: 'Which means what?'

Phone fearer: 'You don't know what I want to talk to you about.'

Me: 'Which means what?'

Phone fearer: 'I've got to pick up the phone haven't I?'

It's at that moment their shoulders drop for two reasons: firstly because they realise they really do have to pick up the phone, and secondly because they realise that they've been missing out on so many opportunities! If I want something I don't leave it to chance and hope an email will get through. I phone that person. And I don't leave a message! (More about that in the actions section of this chapter.)

❝ If I want something I don't leave it to chance and hope an email will get through. I phone that person. And I don't leave a message! ❞

Another business owner phoned and I thought that maybe they had an axe murderer outside their house trying to get in and chop them up into little bits. I was thinking at that moment, 'Don't phone me I'm miles away, phone for a superhero!' In actual fact this business owner was stressed on the phone because we had worked together on creating a strategy to grow their business and one of the actions was to phone past clients and ask them how they were getting on: did they have any current needs, could they get a testimonial for their new website and did they know any one that they would recommend them to? Easy right? Except, although it sounds easy enough to phone a company that this business owner had enjoyed a good relationship with for years, it put genuine fear into them. And so they phoned me. They said, 'I realised I was going to hide behind email again and I thought, I know what Mandie will have to say about that, I've got to phone Mandie and find out how to deal with this!' In these exercises I will share with you what I taught that business owner, which meant I got another squealy phone call, only this time with sheer excitement, because it had worked.

Exercise 1 – Don'ts

The first exercises to do are more about things to remember. Firstly, a few don'ts:

▶ Don't be someone that sends 17 emails and never phones someone. (One business owner I know did!).

▶ Don't play email ping pong. The first lesson I want you to learn is that if you are lobbing the conversation back and forth, that is a good sign. If someone was not interested. Then most humans are quite capable of playing the politician. (Playing the politician is when you don't say what you mean, whether subconsciously or not. If it's subconsciously, your coach will get that out of you and help you deal with that.). You skirt around the real question, the real conversation, and the thing you want to say. You may be capable of speaking for ages without actually saying anything. People who are scared of something will often do this. It's a warning sign for me that something needs addressing when someone does not answer the question I've asked them, but bats around it for ages. I tend to just say 'thank you for being a great politician; however, is there any chance we may get back to the actual question I asked?' Look out for it. It's a good sign that someone doesn't want to answer or deal with what is in front of them, for any number of reasons. So if they have not knocked the conversation out of the court and dismissed you with the 'Thanks but no thanks' i.e., go away email, lobbing is a good sign. So stop sending the endless emails!

▶ Don't just pick up the phone and hope for the best. You wouldn't walk into a presentation that could rocket your success and just wing it would you? So don't just wing it on the phone. In this chapter we are going to look at some skills and your mindset to help you achieve real results. I would like to add that there are people that have devoted their whole lives to just the skill of picking up the phone. And it is becoming such a niche market that one business man is so specialist he only trains dental practice staff on how to communicate on the phone. Thus I would say that a fear of picking up the phone is perfectly normal. As you grew up through your life, most people were taught how to walk, talk, eat, speak, ride a bike, drive a car. However, did anyone teach you how to use the phone effectively?

"Don't just pick up the phone and hope for the best."

Someone may have told you how to answer the phone, but not much past that. Schools now offer interview techniques; however, the ability to speak on the phone that needs surgically removing from teens at meal time, not so much.

So I would like you to remember back to the earlier chapters and be nice to yourself here. This is not your fault. This is a natural fear that has been allowed to escalate over the years. Especially when you consider that so many other forms of communication have come along that mean that we can hide even more.

We've learned some of the 'don'ts' you need to appreciate; however, before you look at the exercises to get a new powerful way to utilise the phone to enable your success, do you accept that the phone has not been your best friend to success? Think for a minute of times in your professional life when phoning people could have been more satisfactory. Being able to spot missed opportunities is really important. You can't change something that is wrong until you can accept that it exists.

"The biggest reason we fear picking up the phone has its roots in the same location as so many other fears, and that starts in your confidence levels."

Before we look at what to say, which is obviously the hardest part for so many, I want you to think about why you fear picking up the phone. The biggest reason we fear picking up the phone has its roots in the same location as so many other fears, and that starts in your confidence levels. That is why this book started by looking at the level of confidence that you have.

(How is that doing by the way? Still on the right side of confidence and not tipping over the edge into arrogance?) If you don't pick up the phone, then your brain is able to play nasty tricks on you and reinforce every bad thought in your mind about you and your ability. Your skills, your success rate, your chances of growth, even your chances of winning at work. Because somewhere in your subconscious brain there are negative beliefs being unchallenged about the outcome of what will happen if you pick up the phone. Now is your chance to deal with them.

The 'What if?' game is a good way of doing this. However, it is only by doing it that you will grow that confidence level. And I still get that this is a scary course of action. Therefore, let's rehearse. At no time do I mean write a script. I personally don't like scripts. I feel they are no good, because the 21st-century business environment is too savvy to so many of the ploys of the past. The sales pitch, the cold call with the hard sell: they're old hat, unpleasant and not good for success. On the other hand, the professional phone call, with the win–win relationship created over the phone in a respectful way, understands how busy the other party is and values that person's time. That is a wondrous thing, and could seriously impact on your success for the better.

So here are some questions you need to answer before you pick up the phone. They are part of your rehearsal. Because picking up the phone is going to be like a knock-out performance. A 5-star show, and you are the star.

▶ **What do I want?** What is the end result that you would like to achieve? Be realistic if for instance you want a new job, new contract or a new customer. It's not prudent to have the attitude of 'show me the money'. It is better to ask for the opportunity to talk about the next step. You only want a 5-minute meeting for instance to discuss how you could be of benefit to the other party.

▶ **What do they want?** What matters to the other party? Think about what they are going to want to hear. And it needs to be more along the lines of 'What's in it for them?', rather than what you want (you will know what you want). How are you going to sell the benefits of the results of this conversation having the result you want? Think about what problems the other party may have. Are they mega busy? Stressed? Overworked? Probably not a good idea to ask for an hour of their time then is it? Word it in a way that makes the other party think, 'This sounds like a no-brainer!'

▶ **What do I want to feel?** How do I want to feel when I put the phone down? Happy, thrilled, excited, scared because the new door to your career success just opened. By imagining how it feels now you can really power up the way you feel before the conversation even starts (and that will help kick fear's butt!)

When you know the I, They and Feel answers it can strengthen your confidence to pick up the phone and, with the other exercise, will help you move onto the right actions to be a success on the phone. However, before you do, one more aspect of the fear of picking up the phone that really kills your success. It's that tiny little word again. How can one word so small, cause so much grief to so many people?

The 'No' word. One of the reasons you don't pick up the phone is for fear of the word 'No'. What if they say 'No'? Horrid, right? No they don't want our company. No they don't want to employ me. No they don't want to place an order. No they don't want to talk about it. But here are a few exercises I want you to do before you move onto Actions to help you break down the 'No' barrier.

"One of the reasons you don't pick up the phone is for fear of the word 'No'."

1 Not all 'No's are bad. 'No's are a chance to learn. To grow. By finding out why someone says 'No' you are able to learn. What made you say 'No'? (Remember 'Why' questions place blame; 'What' questions remove guilt and enable answers.) So ask for people's reasons for the 'No'. And not in a wailing sob of 'Oh why don't you want me!' but in a more professional 'I would appreciate some feedback on your reason for saying "no", to enable me to learn how to get a "yes"'. Practise what your response to a 'No' could be. It's better to be prepared for a 'No'. What feels comfortable to say?

2 Toughen up. 'No's happen. Accept that. And 'No's are good. When successful people look back through their lives they are able to say things like: 'If I hadn't have got sacked from that job, I would never had taken that opportunity and ended up being the success I am today'. Reframe the No's into a 'this is an opportunity for me in disguise'. I have been through some truly shocking experiences in my professional life in the past; however, without them I would not be the business woman I am today. 'No's and failure are massive opportunities, so toughen up. (That is why in Chapter 3 you wrote the list 'Know on a good day what will power up a bad day.') 'No's are part of the process of success. You need them to succeed.

3 The more 'No's you get the closer you are to your 'Yes's. Imagine if I told you you were going to make ten phone calls, and the first five all

said 'No'. Imagine how dejected you would be about picking up the phone the sixth time. What about if the first five all said 'Yes', how excited would you be about picking up the phone the sixth time? It's about your perception. And people that love the phone know this. Learn that 'No's mean you are getting closer to your 'Yes's.

4 It's their loss, not yours. As hard as this one is to accept, when someone says 'No', yes you have things to learn from the 'No', and you can and will learn them. However, it is their loss, and someone else's gain.

5 Not everyone will say 'No'. Don't assume they will. It is a belief that you need to quash. Ask yourself. 'Have I literally asked every single human on the planet?' If not then you've not yet failed have you?

With these 'No' exercises you are able to acquire new ways of thinking around your attitude to the word 'No'.

A – Actions

We've looked at the fear and we've looked at some exercises to help you pick up the phone. It's also going to help you to build confidence to have some core skills too. So here are my top tips for phone success:

G – Gate keepers

I'm often asked how to deal with gate keepers. 'I know *who* I want to speak to, but I just can't get past their PA!' Well the first thing to do is stop trying to! That gate keeper is a person, a human, with emotions and needs and feelings, and it's part of why they get paid to look after the person you are trying to speak to. It was put eloquently to me by my boss many years ago (who I was paid to protect): 'That if I answer that phone it potentially could cost the company work for the staff for a whole day. You are paid to enable me to do my job. Protect me.' I was keen on getting paid, so I protected him. And it was not nice having people speak rudely to me and basically be saying 'Look I don't want you, I want your boss'. So imagine if you stopped trying to get past this person and imagine if you respected this person. Treat every person you speak to with the utmost respect. This should spill over into every aspect of your professional life (you never know who the cleaner has a Friday night drink with!). If you are kind and respectful to the person who answers the phone, do you think you are more likely to get a chance of finding out how to move the conversation forward.

> *"Treat every person you speak to with the utmost respect (you never know who the cleaner has a Friday night drink with!)."*

Ask questions like:

► 'I appreciate I will not be able to speak to Mrs X today, could you tell me the best way to communicate an idea I've had that could save our company £10,000 a year on our expenses account. Tell Mrs X it's research I did on my own time.' Now any PA that values their job will want to impress and keep their boss happy right? Even if they don't show them what you suggest they do. What is the chance they may give it 2 minutes of their time to see if it's more junk or if it's really useful to the company?

► 'Hello, may I ask whom I'm speaking to please?' Getting a name is good for many reasons. Firstly it says. I don't want to get past you. You are the person that matters to me. (That just improved your chances!) Also when you follow up, it means you can start the conversation with that person's name.

Never forget whose ear the gate keeper has. Even if you fail, still be polite and respectful at all times.

O – Opening

A big mistake many people make when they pick up the phone is they say 'Is now a good time to talk or are you busy?' You just gave that person the perfect out of the conversation. It is far better to ask a question (and again remember to practise this so you find a question that feels natural to you) like: 'Is now a good time to speak or shall I call back at 2.30 today or perhaps tomorrow at 10 am?' This is good for the following reasons: 1) you are appreciating that this person is busy and respecting their time by getting permission to talk, 2) you are making them aware that they are not going to be so lucky as to get out of the conversation without you calling back, and bonus 3) you've told them that it will be imminent and you are making it look like their choice as to when the conversation will be.

A – Acting and answerphones

Firstly, when it comes to answerphones – they are the equivalent of a phone's email. Are you really going to trust this big opportunity to get lost in a phone's email? I've heard successful business owners say: 'Don't bother leaving me an answerphone message, I won't listen to it.' So why would you take that risk with your success?. If you can't get through to the person you wish to speak to a handful of times and you really have to leave a message, pre-plan it, and know what you want to say. Know what your desired outcome is. Don't just wing it and have the attitude of 'Oh it's fine I will just leave my name and number and they will call me back message'. Where's the incentive for them to call you back in that?

Secondly, the way you act on the phone is really important. Stand, don't sit: it impacts on your performance Remember we want a standing ovation not a mediocre performance. You want to act like you are supposed to be on that phone with that person. 'Hi Ann, how are you?' In business it's all too often that we forget how we know this person on the end of the phone. So act like you belong.

And along with acting, act like yourself. Don't try and be someone else on the phone. It will seep out and it tends to show up in conversations as gut instinct to third parties that makes people question if they are really interested. And that's the last thing you want to happen. So stay natural and true to yourself.

**❝Don't try and be someone else on the phone . . .
stay natural and true to yourself.❞**

Remembering to breathe will help here too. A pause in a conversation can feel really scary. However, it's good for you to enable you to keep calm. And it's good for the person on the other end of the line to be able to process what you are saying. Not only that, a lot of people dislike silences and so they are likely to fill it with talking too. Which means they are likely to agree to what you want to get you off the phone quicker!

L – Listen

It's not just your breathing you need to listen to. How do they sound? Do they sound stressed or relaxed? Is there the sound of a keyboard being tapped? Are they running the tap or driving a car? Do you feel that you have their undivided attention? Do you think they are stressed? Do you think they are interested? By being a more aware listener, you will be able to assess how the conversation is progressing.

Secret language is powerful on the phone. Clients who think they can hide on the phone quickly realise they cannot. Our body language seeps into the way we communicate. Look out for the signs in your recipient, and be aware of their choice of language. You can then use their own style of language and even use some of their words back in the conversation. By doing this you showcase that they are being listened to. For instance: 'I appreciate you are happy working with A & P Solutions, and it's great that they are able to deliver the services to you under budget each month. Does it matter to you that you learn about new developments in this field to further cut costs? Is that something that A & P Solutions are able to do?'

S – Study

Before you even pick up the phone, to really fight the fear, know who you are phoning. Research them. Take a moment to search them online. What is the company's vision and mission statement? Names are very important and companies more and more have pages showcasing their staff. Take the time to study before your call.

And if you take these actions you may have noticed they spell out the acronym GOALS (well, I do like an easy way for you to be able to remember how to make picking up the phone actually happen). You should be aiming for relationships. Not just any kind of relationships, but win–win respectful relationships. Because:

▶ You don't know who this person on the end of the phone knows.
▶ You can't dictate when someone is ready to do business with you or give you that opportunity; however, you can have a say in whom they choose to give that opportunity to.

By building win–win respectful relationships and effectively following up you will be able to deal with your fear of the phone and make it a distant memory.

❝You can't dictate when someone is ready to do business with you or give you that opportunity; however, you can have a say in whom they choose to give that opportunity to.❞

R – Results

When you master this chapter I would love to see the look on your face the first time you put the phone down and smile, thinking, 'Wow, I did it!' In fact get in touch on social media and tell me! I've seen people fix this and ask themselves 'How could I let this fear stand in the way of my success for so long?' That can be disheartening; however, don't let it be. It's the results you want to focus on, by doing that you will be able to give yourself even more confidence to tackle more fears, and boost your confidence and self-belief even further. Which will be great for your success rate.

One business owner had a habit of hiding behind emails and never picking up the phone. Actually it was worse than that. They actually would send one email and then leave it for months hoping that eventually by osmosis or magic unicorns or something else just as random, the dream contract would land on this company's doorstep. It didn't, until we worked together. We worked out a strategy to go back to past clients and ask for new opportunities to work together if they'd assumed that they weren't going to be needed any more and so didn't get in touch with anyone. We created some structure to their offerings and when we were finishing up I for a moment foolishly assumed that they were going to phone them to get the ball rolling on this process. And in one little sigh this business owner gave themselves away. (See the power a sigh can have?) I questioned what that sigh meant. They explained that they didn't feel comfortable phoning this organisation, and that possibly it would be more prudent to send an email or letter and then follow that up in a few weeks. That set my alarm bells ringing! We looked at the results that not picking up the phone had created and I asked the question: 'So tell me, if I came back in six weeks' time and said I was chopping off your little finger if you had not phoned them, would you have done it?' The business owner looked at me in horror. 'Of course I would have phoned them!' they said. It helped them appreciate that behind their politician response and fear if there was a big enough motive to pick up the phone, then they would do it. And it wasn't the joy and happiness at securing a dream contract, at securing the company's future for the next year. It was the sheer horror and pain that they could feel. (I hasten to add I finished the session by saying 'at no time would I ever hurt you'.) And do you know what, it wasn't in six weeks that this business owner had phoned them: it was within the week. Guess what the impact of that has been to their business; not just for that contract but even to this very day.

"If someone says 'give me a call', assume they mean it."

Results of picking up the phone are powerful. And as many good stories I can share I can sadly share the negative results too. The business woman that lost out on a great opportunity because she didn't pick up the phone and make the call that was expected of her after a brief conversation. The scariest thing is the assumptions people make. If someone says 'give me a call', assume they mean it. Remember that 'No's are good for you. And power up your results by assuming that when someone says, 'I'd love to know more' – phone them. Winning at work is the prize; don't let fear take it out of your hands.

9

I don't want to look stupid

F – Fear

The fear of looking stupid has haunted us since we were little. There will be a time at some point in everyone's past when they can remember being embarrassed. Ask your friends on social media when they were last embarrassed and they will be able to regale you with a great story that years later is good for around the table chuckles over drinks but at the time was mortifying. We've all got one. But this goes beyond that. The fear of not wanting to look stupid can really damage your success. It can be a defining factor in your career. It can be what separates you from other people in your profession; what rockets their success and railroads yours.

> **The fear of not wanting to look stupid can really damage your success. It can be a defining factor in your career.**

Have you ever:

▶ Sat in a meeting and thought 'that slide is wrong' and said nothing?

▶ Wanted to ask a question but feared to?

▶ Spent years in the office with someone you don't know the name of?

▶ Struggled with something because you don't want to ask the person that handles those type of things (they always look so busy!)?

▶ Been in a meeting and lost the thread of the conversation and been too embarrassed to say anything so just sat there?

▶ Not made eye contact for fear of being asked to comment?

If any of the above are true for you then there is a good chance that the fear of looking stupid is impacting on you.

The place I see this happening the most impacting on success is when I'm training. People striving for more success have given up their time to work with me and a small group of other like-minded individuals and it's not until the refreshment break that this person will sidle forward and subtly ask me a question like a secret agent on covert operations. Usually it will be a question that relates to something much earlier in the day. And that impacts on how they've interpreted the whole session up until this moment. That is why I tell people: 'There is no such thing as a stupid question. If you don't know the answer to something, that is an obstacle to your success.'

> **There is no such thing as a stupid question. If you don't know the answer to something, that is an obstacle to your success.**

Before we tackle that fear, we have to be able to appreciate that it is a fear and what impact it has on success. You can't fix something until you know it exists, right? Above are a few examples of how that fear can manifest. Can you imagine how it could feel for you? Do you feel confident to step out of your comfort zone and get the answers you need? This is what this chapter looks at: the confidence to override the fear that says 'I can't do that; I will look stupid'. If it's allowed to fester for long enough it can escalate and it can influence the way you think other people see you too. And that is why the next chapter is 'I can't stop scrutinising what people think'. They link beautifully together. Although the current chapter can stand alone to really power up success, reading the chapters together gives you a powerful tool kit. So firstly we will work on feeling the internal confidence to act in a way that empowers your self-reliance and overrides the fear to get the answers you need for success. And then in the next chapter we will deal with the way you feel about what other people think about you and the constant barrage of thought that could be impacting on you.

It's an odd one to fear asking questions. When we were little everything was a question:

▶ Why is the sky blue?

▶ Why are mints minty?

▶ Why is the grass green?

▶ Why is water wet?

▶ Why is the night dark?

Endless. We never feared questions as young children. In fact, we relished in the endless questions. It enabled us to form our world. It wasn't just the questions that were answered that helped us form our world: the person we asked and the amount of time that was given to us helped us feel a certain way too.

As we've grown up it changes; we learn that endless questions are considered impolite. People will perceive us in a different way if we constantly ask questions, won't they? In the work place, once you are over the 'new' stage (when a few questions are tolerated and accepted) you are assumed to know everything you need to know. People muddle on through. Thinking things like:

▶ I didn't like to trouble them.

▶ They always look so busy.

▶ It's not appropriate to ask for help on that.

▶ I think everyone else knows how to do that, so its assumed I know too.

And yet unless you take yourself out of your comfort zone, you are agreeing to remain in the dark, trapped in your comfort zone agreeing to an obstacle to success.

Another reason that people fear speaking up and risk looking stupid is because when you are looking to win at work it's a tough game, right? As someone so eloquently put it to me: 'It's war out there.' Everyone is after the same job. On paper we all look the same, so don't dare risk showing any sign of weakness. They'd stab you in the back if the opportunity came up. 'I can't show any flaw, that would be their opportunity to attack.' Someone told me that if there are a number of dogs living together and one dog becomes very old and poorly, even though it has been the top dog (the alpha) the strongest dog will fight for supremacy and shove the weak older alpha out. Essentially sending it away to die. I get the idea that many people feel that by risking asking for what you need and risking looking stupid you're fearful that some alpha is going to come and snap at your heels until you get out of that office and never darken their doorstep ever again!

I know my analogies probably make you say, 'Don't be so daft Mandie'; however, in essence, when we don't ask for what we need, that is what we are doing. We push people on to these evil pedestals where they will be ready to attack at the first sign of weakness. In actual fact in my experience never have I come across so many people prepared to give other people a little bit of their time to mentor, coach and support them to get the results that they want. You just need to have the guts to ask for it. And that is a big ask. It's a devious, sly, subtle fear that can hide away and just hold you back enough. You know how they say give 110%? Whether you agree that it is possible to give more than 100% or not, the point is that you could be missing out on the winning edge because of this sly fear. In the exercise of this chapter we will look at how to get out of this comfort zone that traps you. Whether you want to carefully creep out or jump so far you can't see it any more.

"Never have I come across so many people prepared to give other people a little bit of their time to mentor, coach and support them to get the results that they want."

E – Examples and exercises

Example

Long before I stepped out of my comfort zone, when I had far less confidence than I do now, I can remember that I was sat in a beautiful venue with 10 other very lucky people, all looking to improve their career success. We were about to learn from a business expert, journalist and broadcaster for women. It was a great opportunity and we all paid money to be there. And yet within a few sentences of the training I realised I was lost. I felt rather stupid, because my background was in small business and not corporate business, and her natural style was way above me. Her language contained acronyms and phrases I'd never heard in my life. How was I to grow my business and to become a successful business coach if I couldn't understand what an expert was trying to teach me? I had two choices:

1 Sit quietly, write every word down and hope I could translate it online when I got home and make sense of it all.

2 Put my hand up and override the humiliation to get the answers I needed.

I chose option two. And as embarrassing as it was at the time, and yes there were a couple of people who looked down their noses at me, it was definitely the right thing to do. This expert was just wonderful. I will always remember her as one of the nicest people I've ever learnt from, because she instantly ditched the jargon. Told me about a great website called Business Balls.com and I learnt a ton of great ideas and advice. What is more, I noticed a good few shoulders noticeably drop when I asked my embarrassing question of 'I'm really sorry to be dense, but I don't know what these acronyms mean – my professional background was in SMEs.' And in the break it was a great icebreaker with people thanking me for helping them get more out of the day! If I had hidden my lack of knowledge on the meaning of corporate acronyms, I would never have learnt about Business Balls or what a wonderful trainer and educator she was as well as a first-rate broadcaster.

Another person who feared looking stupid had a shiny career with many accolades, but found themselves in new territory, facing redundancy and a new business. This person's burning ambitions didn't include taking over the world any more. Their focus had changed, and yet how could they tell people that? How could they get the dream contracts and take their business to where they wanted to take it if they didn't go for every contract and kill themselves working 24 hours a day? They wanted a different life. And they couldn't see how that was possible because that 'just wasn't done.' By working together using the tools in this chapter, this person was able to stop hiding who they were, be honest about what they wanted for themselves and their professional lives and get it.

Exercises

The exercises in this chapter assume it's becoming second nature to play the 'What if?' game and the negative spiral is utilised to help you understand what you are agreeing to. By getting into good habits and allowing yourself to use these exercises in every area of your life and naturally throughout your working day, you will be able to see what your choices are going to result in and how you are impacting on your success. In comparison, you are also able to see how you are damaging your success by not taking action and gaining momentum by playing these games. You are far more likely to get results if you've really made yourself experience the true horror of how bad things could be. Remember we are ultimately motivated into action by the bad stuff.

❝You are far more likely to get results if you've really made yourself experience the true horror of how bad things could be.❞

Exercise 1 – Reframing your comfort zones

Before we deal with your comfort zone let's reframe your view on yours, so you hate yours so much you're compelled to take action:

1 I want you to think of the thing you fear looking stupid about. And I want you to see this as a comfort zone that you feel there is no need to change.

2 Now visualise your comfort zone as a duvet you are nuzzled up in on a winter's night. You can hear the rain and wind, thrashing against your window. You've nowhere in the world you need to be. Your loved ones are all safe, and you feel warm and snuggly.

3 Now imagine you are still wrapped up in your duvet but it's a hot summer's night. The duvet is still all around your legs, it's hot and you feel claustrophobic, and sweaty. You are trapped, and the more you try to wiggle free the tighter the duvet has you. The sweat dripping down your

legs only enables the duvet to grip you tighter and tighter; that is what a comfort zone does. It can feel like a good place to be, until you realise what it is doing to you. Then you are trapped there. Since we just reframed yours into a damaging hindrance to success, shall we get rid of it?

Now I want you to grab Post-it notes or a small pad and on each small piece of paper write a belief you hold about the way you feel about looking stupid. Remember our statements from the start of the chapter. What beliefs do you hold? For instance:

▶ 'When I ask Fiona for help I know she thinks I'm paid too much if I can't even do this.'

▶ 'If I bumble my words in a phone call then I look stupid and why would they want us?'

Write every thought down, however silly or negative. This is for your eyes only. Now bin the lot! Take a moment to reread every statement you made about yourself and the beliefs you hold, and then rip it up, screw it up, but bin it. Physically get rid of it.

Do you remember in Chapter 5 we talked about finding your natural style? I want you to explore and really know yours, thus *When it comes to trying new things what is your natural style?* (This doesn't have to be work related; however, by knowing how you naturally tackle new things it can help you handle comfort zones around the fear of looking stupid.) For instance:

▶ Do you like to jump straight in and have a go?

▶ Do you like to see other people doing it first?

▶ Would you rather research first?

Take those ideas into the situation that risks you looking stupid and damaging your success. What could move you into positive action? For instance, with new technology that comes into the home my approach is: 'Play with it, do it and learn from my actions and my mistakes, then ask cleverer people than me that like instruction manuals.' My mindset says 'I accept that I lack patience in the work place and I trust people that have a passion for I.T. and technology. I play to my strengths. And accept and work on my weaknesses.' This statement at no time damages my success rate. I'm accepting I'm prepared to learn new skills; however, when I'm busy I know I would rather pay someone else to do the techie stuff. I don't look or feel stupid. So what would your actions and thoughts be saying to power up your results?

"I play to my strengths. And accept and work on my weaknesses."

A – Actions

This may feel like a silly fear, and one to skim read. However, I've seen this fear physically stop people from taking the actions that could rocket success. So why, when you are on the path to what you want, would you allow anything to stay in your way, however small.

With the actions to take, the big thing to remember about the fear of looking stupid is you have allowed the fear to hide out in your subconscious for years, completely unchallenged. Unless you are a 'Get so far out of your comfort zone you can't see it any more' kind of person (like myself) then it is not going to happen overnight. So here are a few actions to take that will ensure you get the results you want.

> **"The big thing to remember about the fear of looking stupid is you have allowed the fear to hide out in your subconscious for years, completely unchallenged. "**

▶ Be respectful of your natural style. If you don't do big gestures then don't stroll into the office Monday morning and stand on the table and shout, 'For the record I don't even know what a form 7RJ1 is, how to fill it in or what to do with it!'– that is going to do very little to boost your confidence. The right actions will keep you motivated to do more and more. So be respectful of you.

▶ Accept that sometimes fear can manifest itself as physical things and it's not to be feared. The first time I publicly spoke at an international speaker and trainer Mark Rhodes event I had to put my notes down on the lectern because I was shaking with nerves so badly! I accepted the reasons why – I was excited to be asked to speak at such a prestigious event so early in my coaching career to my target audience, I wanted to perform well. I'd read that actors and musicians actually see nerves prior to a performance as a good thing. It means that the show matters to them and they want to do their best. I read somewhere: 'It's not stage fright it's performance energy.' So the physical things you experience when you take on these new things are perfectly normal.

▶ The more you do it, the better it will get. It won't always be perfect. However, every time you do this it will get easier. You learn from your action and improve your performance, constantly noticing what worked, what didn't and what could be improved on.

R – Results

The fear of looking stupid is a tricky one. It can manifest itself as so many other fears and thus not get dealt with effectively. And we can deal with those fears and still leave this one lurking in the background ready to strike or resurface in a new format if you don't find a way to kick its butt.

> **"The fear of looking stupid is a tricky one. It can manifest itself as so many other fears and thus not get dealt with effectively."**

I once worked with a client who feared looking stupid if they phoned a repeat customer to ask for more money to do the same contract they'd done for them in the past. Without the renegotiation the client was in effect agreeing to work for a very low figure and it could seriously damage their profit margin, and put the business's future in jeopardy. (This, however, was something they had only become aware of as we had worked together and so repricing was really their only option, if they were to continue working with this customer. The business needed growth and increased profitability and through the coaching process we had crunched the numbers and discovered the terms were not viable in the long term. However, to ask for more money . . . ?) As much as they appreciated this, it was difficult to comprehend how they could phone this large organisation that they had really valued working with and basically say, 'We want more, a lot more money to do what we have already done for you'. It had been an amazing coup for this company to get the job in the first place: how could they risk rocking the boat? This was professional suicide! 'This could ruin our reputation in the industry!' 'We could look very foolish!' Helping them to see what they were agreeing to was not enough. However, I made it personal. Because I had worked with this client over a few months, we had already worked out the company's long-term goals and I knew the business owner's values and I knew the hot buttons and fears that they had. I had worked with this director and knew their core values; what drove them to success. The conversation went a little like this:

'So basically you are like a supermodel?'

'I beg your pardon?' They asked in horror and disdain, because I knew that this kind of shallowness would not sit comfortably with them. This person was an incredibly professional, corporate business owner who 'didn't suffer fools lightly' and I knew this kind of superficial profession of the fashion world was the furthest removed from my client that you could possibly imagine – remember *to get out of a comfort zone, sometimes you have to feel the uncomfortableness of the environment you are in.*

'A supermodel.' I expanded. 'Someone that doesn't even get out of bed for anything less than £7,000 a day. Which is, in essence, what we are saying. You won't negotiate, because it's below you. It's beneath you.'

'That is not what we are saying at all!' They argued immediately. Seeing the sarcasm that I was giving them.

'Okay, so what are you saying?' They sat back in their chair, squirmed and gave me a knowing 'Oh-Mandie's-got-me-sussed look' and said, 'Fine I will call them.'

You see how feeling stupid can hide out on your pathway to success? Don't let it. What is great news with the Director in this story is that with the right coaching I know that they renegotiated with that company a far better contract that was more profitable for them, with fewer hours, so they were freer for more opportunities too. They really proved they could win at work.

I'd like to close this chapter with two statements that could be good to remember to enable you to practise the exercises and take the action to get the results, and they are:

▶ People like honesty.
▶ If you don't ask, you don't get.

10

I can't stop scrutinising what people are thinking

F – Fear

The fear of what another person is thinking slips into our mir
all the time, sometimes harmlessly, but sometimes witl
knock-on effect that damages your chances of winning at wc

At its worst I've seen it create a level of procrastination that stops a pers
from taking any action at all. To wander from one action to another, w
no real purpose or focus.

The 21st century is a world where there is literally a camera in every roo
In our phones, laptops, our cars, at the end of our street, in our offices a
every aspect of our lives. Thus people document, comment and share ev
ything and anything. So you can be privy to another person's viewpoin
any time of day of night on any subject you can imagine. Basically anyor
thoughts can be practically projected into your brain. No wonder we o
feel like we can hear their thoughts all of the time.

If you are looking to succeed at work, it's highly likely you are aiming
grow an effective and well-managed network too. To do that you neec
know people, and you do this by getting out there and communicat
with people. That in itself has its own glut of fears, skills and minds
needed to be handled, managed and dealt with to succeed. The downs
of learning all of that and knowing the benefits of an effective networl
the fear of what they could all know about you:

> ❝The downside of knowing the benefits
> of an effective network is the fear of what
> they could all know about you.

- ▶ 'What if they were all talking about you?'
- ▶ 'I wonder what Mr X really thinks of me?'
- ▶ 'I wonder if they think I got this job because they wanted to m.
  the company look good or because I was really the right person
  the job.'
- ▶ 'They think I'm too old, too young for this job.'

The things we tell ourselves are expanded into a million other nega
thoughts when we imagine what everyone else might be thinking too.

This fear can manifest itself in far more than just thought. It can rip
through every aspect of your life and cause repercussions that stop y
taking action, lead to procrastination and even make you question y

own judgement and ability. It's almost as if all those voices are given permission to take up residence in your head.

E – Examples and exercises

Example

I met one person looking to get to the top, who wasn't going to look back, who had grand ambitions, who had already achieved so much at such a young age. This person suddenly seemed to stagnate and freeze solid in their career, just as they were stepping forward to the next level which looked to be very exciting and hold a lot of possibility. When we worked together they were very honest about what their family and friends kept saying to them: 'Was this really what you want at this stage in your life', 'You've achieved so much, this just doesn't seem to make sense to us', 'Shouldn't you go back to the company you were working for'. This person realised the constant talk wherever they went was beginning to affect their mindset; and not just their mindset. As we talked through the issues they found they were facing they were able to see where it was impacting on their actions too. I think the scariest impact you can see of other people's thoughts on yourself is the way that they can impact on the actions you take and the way you speak to other people: it literally can make you speak in a different way and get a different result.

Think about that for a moment. Instead of being in a meeting and being like a healthy equation that you prepare and that you know will work so that you feel comfortable and confident in what you will say and do to get the results you want, you walk in, fumble and fall over your words. You forget what you wanted to say, what you want to get and end up feeling like a fool who missed the point of the meeting.

Another way that I've seen this fear impact on a person's ability to succeed is when it comes to action. However, it does not manifest itself as a fear, it manifests itself as procrastination. I know someone who was so worried about what one person was thinking that it literally stopped them taking action on their business. It stopped them in their tracks. How could they confront this person? How could they deal with this person? What would they say? It whirred around in their head at night stopping them from sleeping and it blocked their brain's ability to think during the working day so they couldn't concentrate on anything else either. That was the reason they came to me, because they knew something was wrong; however, they

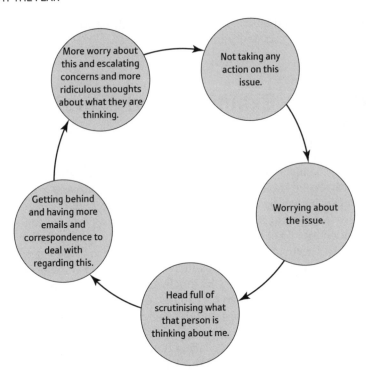

didn't know what. By working together, we were able to see what their negative circle was (see figure).

The good news is that by becoming aware of the process that they were allowing to happen they were able to deal with it really fast. Unlike fears like public speaking or phone fear, where some genuine skills need to be learnt as well as changing your mindset and your beliefs, this fear can be dealt with just by dealing with what you think. I know the word 'just' is a bit of a stretch because it is something you may have done for a long time. However, that is the joy about the mindset. With the right support and the right actions, you can change it.

66Unlike fears like public speaking or phone fear, this fear can be dealt with just by dealing with what you think.99

Exercise 1 – Power goals 2

The first exercise I want you to do could change your life for ever. That is not a flippant over-exaggeration. This is said from the experience of the people I've worked with. I've always told my clients: 'This is not therapy, this is coaching. Let's find out what's wrong and sort it.' When you learn the true power of this exercise it can really help you in so many fears.

Have you ever spotted a person across a crowded room and thought, 'you are the one for me' and not been able to see anyone else? Or have you ever been driving along and only one car is catching your eye, because it's your dream car? It's that constant ability to be so focused and intent on your end target that nothing else comes into view; and that includes someone else's thoughts.

Setting goals that are so focused and clear you feel like you've already achieved them can really help. Let's look at how that is achieved. I could talk about creating SMART (Specific Measurable Achievable Realistic and Time measurable) goals; however, even that doesn't go far enough.

> **"Setting goals that are so focused and clear you feel like you've already achieved them can really help."**

To stay so focused so that you are like a runaway train, never losing momentum you need to do the following:

1 Know that the goal is aligned to your core values (and you know how to check that, right?)

2 Write down everything you could do to achieve that goal. And here is the key. Regardless of time constraints, skill gaps, money shortages, reality gaps; the fact that you don't know the said movie star; the fact that unicorns don't exist. Don't let anything get sidetracked. Write anything and everything down. When you allow your creative brain to go wild with any ideas that pop into your head, then your brain can really explore the depths of your subconscious for ideas that might be lurking in there. Remember, if you've been so busy stressing about what everyone else is thinking your brain has no space to think of creative or clever ideas about how to achieve what you really want. This exercise frees your mind. Quite literally. So if you are constantly worrying about what that person at work thinks of you, write down what you want to be achieving, not what you want to be thinking about that person. This is an internal, not an external goal. Does that person factor in your goal? Will you be that person's boss? If so, how? When? If that person is not directly related to that goal, do not add them to your long list of possibilities to achieve your goal.

> **"It's only by really getting to grips with the absurd and daft ideas that you are able to embrace the ideas that could be powerful."**

3   When you have written a long list of what you could do, write a second page of what you could do. By writing for longer and letting your brain become totally immersed in this exercise it will create more ideas and that is where the stronger ideas are; the first ideas you write down are the ones that your mind has been churning around in your head and keeping you awake at night. It's only by really getting to grips with the absurd and daft ideas that you are able to embrace the ideas that could be powerful. For instance, it may sound mad to talk about unicorns, magic or blowing up phones to get a bit of peace and quiet; however, from mad ideas you can create sensible ones. No its not realistic to blow up all the phones in the office; however, it is realistic to use sound-deadening head phones, or to get to work early or to put your phone on silent, isn't it? Can you see why it is important to write more? This can be tricky. So stick with it. If you find it hard to be creative and it's not your natural state, here are some suggestions to take you deeper into creative goal ideas:

▶   'I could quit working here and set up my own business, even though I would need millions in funding (that would magically get given to me) to head hunt the top five people in the industry (they'd all get brainwashed into coming with me) and need to magically gain the skills of the top negotiators in the world to get the contracts we would need.' (It is crazy but go with it; crazy ideas, allow your creative brain to think freely.)

▶   'I could become the world's first self-employed person doing this. Even though the industries we work in don't allow this, I would use the magic powers to make that all change.' (Many industries have had change thrust upon them, it happened because someone turned around and said 'Yes, but why?' let your creative mind ask the 'Yes, but why?')

4   When you have a really long list, allow your brain to look through the crazy ideas. And *feel* what feels interesting (still don't allow your conscious 'that it's impossible' part of your brain to take over). The daft ones may make you laugh; however, they could actually have grains of good ideas in them. Things do not stay the same. Remember that, because when we make assumptions about what people are thinking, it can impact on the actions we take. So by creating clear goals that are internal and are not based on someone else but ourselves we are able to stay focused on them. With your mind on the ones that interest you, come up with a list of a maximum of three. Remember too many goals is as bad as too much thought. It causes lack of actions because we can become overwhelmed.

**"For each goal know what you could
do to achieve the end result. "**

5 For each goal know what you could do to achieve the end result. Keep the crazy ideas in there, because they can be the ones that can spur real ideas to surface from a deeper level of consciousness.

6 Of the ideas you have created, what actions will you take?

7 The biggest issue I see in most goals is the assumptions you are making. What assumptions are you making around this goal? Do you assume that the boss just wants you to turn up to work and do your job and not make suggestions? 'He wouldn't be interested in my idea to save the company 15% on HR costs.' Do you assume that the amazing inspirational business speaker you just heard doesn't need an accountant so you won't tell them about how you could help them (not sell at them; in the 21st century there is no need to sell 'at' people!) Have you assumed that the person looking across the room at you in the networking event is giving you dirty looks and hates you. Or that they are envious of you and are desperate to know how you do it. 'How I do it? How I do what? I'm was thinking the same about you!'

8 Assumptions are a bigger obstacle to success and we will tackle them in more detail in the next chapter; however, in this chapter if you don't know, don't assume. When it comes to what people are thinking, that is their concern not yours. Stay focused on your work goals.

9 Stay focused. If you create a clearly defined goal and a course of action that you constantly and effectively work on, eradicating the assumptions that cause you to procrastinate and waiver from positive thought and strong conviction, then you will be able to stay focused. However, the most successful people will tell you that every success has a good few dollops of stress and failure. What will you do to stay focused? Remember that you need to know on a good day how to deal with a bad day? Remember the people, the places, the words and the actions that will keep you in a positive mindset to keep you focused.

Exercise 2 – The bubble game

Another exercise that is powerful to remember when you over-scrutinise other people's thoughts is that other people are actually as busy with their own thoughts as you are with yours: and I can prove this. I've done a lot of training and speaking engagements around public speaking fears and skills. One of the areas it is feared the most is at a networking event. In a room full of professionals, I will point out the person sat furthest to the left of me and say, 'Right now this person is the most frightened in the room', and everyone sniggers.

Then I explain that when it comes to public speaking and you tell every
that we are now all going to do our elevator pitches and we are going to s
on the right of the room, the person on the left of the room, is thinking, '
no, I'm last!.' This basically means they won't hear what any of you are say
because they have got at least half an hour to be worried about public spe
ing and what they are going to say. How do I know this? Because that u
to be me! And that always gets a laugh, because it's so true. When I've as
the audience 'what kind of things do you find yourself thinking when y
are the person sat in the audience instead of on stage, people have share

▶ 'I'm glad it's not me up there.'

▶ 'I could never do that.'

▶ 'If it looks like that microphone is coming near me, I'm going to p
tend I need to take a call.'

▶ 'I can't think straight because I know it's me next.'

I once read we would rather be in the coffin at a funeral than at the fr
giving the eulogy!

“We would rather be in the coffin at a funeral than at the front giving the eulogy!

So when you take that into the context of scrutinising what people thi
and you've been asked to think, and your mind is awash with 'They th
I'm rubbish', 'They are looking at the spot on my nose', 'I bet they
wondering why I've been asked to do this instead of Mrs X', in actual f
they are all thinking: 'Wow what a relief it's not me up there!'

Imagine if you played the bubble game the next time the fear was creep
into your head you imagine little speech bubbles appearing above peop
heads. What would really be in them? I'm sorry to burst your bubble, I
none of us are that important in other people's heads that they are actua
thinking about us all day. So what would be in other people's speech b
bles magically appearing above their heads?

▶ 'I wonder what's for tea?'

▶ 'Did I lock the back door?'

▶ 'I don't think I turned my phone on silent, that could
embarrassing.'

▶ 'That feels like a hole in my tights, I better subtly check that befor
stand up.'

▶ 'I think that is Mr Smith over there. I hear there is position going in l
department, I ought to go and have a chat when this is over.'

▶ 'How come he looks calm and confident speaking to us and I'm nervous just being in the room. Is everyone staring at me?'

Exercise 3 – Write it, rant it, bin it

Lastly, when it comes to scrutinising what people are thinking, there will be occasions when you need to do something about it. Not all thoughts in someone else's head can be ignored. It could be your gut instinct needs listening to; that what you think is being said is being said and that it is impacting on your ability to win at work. This final exercise is called Write it, Rant it, Bin it.

I love the stories I've read about great people – Ghandi, Mother Teresa, Winston Churchill and so many others. I also get saddened by the fact that so many people share their quotes on social media; however, they do not share their *actions*. You see all great moments in time came about by what someone *did* rather than what they *said*. They may have started with what they *thought*, but it was their *actions* that mattered. It was their actions that changed history. Not what came out of their mouths. That is important to remember for the 'Write it, Rant it, Bin it' exercise.

▶ Think what you think is being said?
▶ How is it impacting on you?
▶ How is it impacting on your success?
▶ I don't want you to confront this person in the real world (yet).
▶ I want you to literally write everything you can about what you think it is doing to you. What you think it is causing to happen to your life, your success and your future.
▶ Now get really angry about it.
▶ How dare they!
▶ How dare they damage your success!
▶ How dare they be so outrageous as to impact on what you want in life, this is disgusting, this is abhorrent, this a travesty of justice!

You still feel that they are at risk of impacting on your ability to win at work. This is one of the rare occasions where you will have to confront and challenge a thought: and not just in your mind – you may have to consider that you challenge this person in real life. As scary as this can be, it does bring closure – one way or the other. It does allow you to create space for your goals. To clear the air and to know where you stand, in my experience.

How does it feel now? Do you feel still wronged and disrespected? At this stage one of two things should happen. Either:

▶ You will realise that regardless of what is going on in that person's head, you have complete control of what is going on in your head and as such you can stay focused on your career and goals and not allow someone else's thoughts to impact on yours again. In which case you can bin everything you wrote down and thought. They are their thoughts, not yours. And as you don't have their experience, life, skills or values, how could that person be impacting on your goals?

▶ You still feel that they are at risk of impacting on your ability to win at work. This is one of the rare occasions where you will have to confront and challenge a thought - and not just in your mind. You may have to consider challenging this person in real life. As scary as this can be, it does bring closure – one way or the other. It does allow you to create space for your goals, to clear the air and to know where you stand – in my experience. Structuring what you wish to say without emotion but with clarity and a calm manner will enable you to get your message across, and it leads to both parties knowing where they stand. I've seen this lead to the other party feeling threatened and making the challenger's life rather difficult (although that challenger is now in charge of a team of 45+ people including the other party). I've seen the scrutineering stop immediately because it was a complete misunderstanding and I've seen people end up collaborating on projects because it turns out they have so much in common. It is without doubt a scary prospect; however, winning at work does necessitate challenging times when you have to really raise your game and do things that scare you. If you apply the same rules of 'create a powerful focused goal', 'have the right level of self-confidence' and 'believe that you can succeed' then you will move forward.

In which case you can bin everything you wrote down and thought: they are their thoughts, not yours. And as such you don't have their experience, life skills or values, so how could that person be impacting on your goals? Crazy to let them right? Let's get on with winning at work!

 # A – Action

The trouble with scrutinising what everyone else thinks is that you end up so absorbed in everyone else's thoughts there is no time to absorb and explore your own. Which means that you end becoming rather average. People that win at work stay focused on what they want; they are not constantly consumed with the contents of everyone else's head. Don't get confused with not caring about other people. They do care about other people, but they don't become consumed with their thoughts. Do you want to be average or exceptional?

Winning at work needs you to stay focused. And if you want to beat this fear, then stay focused, because you quickly learn that there is no room for worrying about what everyone else is thinking when you are concentrating on your own success. Suddenly everyone else's thoughts stay just where they are, and you can get on with winning at work.

Look around you at what impacts on you. If you are super obsessed with other people's thoughts, is this reinforced in an undesirable way by social media? It's your choice who you talk to online and what conversations you have. If you are really affected, do you really need your phone by your side and turned on all the time? Remember if you are trying to break a negative habit that means you scrutinise what everyone is thinking about you. What are you agreeing to, by reading your social media streams?

Who can you trust? Sometimes the way we think about something can drastically change just by changing our thoughts. Who could you talk to? – and this is not to have a moaning and berating session of 'She said this' and 'I think she meant this'. This is to share your concerns and get confidential independent feedback, ideally from someone that you can trust to be a mentor and give advice. It can be surprising how a different viewpoint can flip your beliefs about what you are thinking on their head.

And lastly I can't stress enough, stay focused on what you want. The goals, the ambitions. The thoughts you want in your head instead of the ones that you don't. Staying focused will protect your brain space from the negative thoughts.

"Staying focused will protect your brain space from the negative thoughts."

 # R – Results

We've touched on the damage that allowing this fear to play out in your professional life can have; however, I can testify first-hand how easy it is to lose track of what your real goals are, when you become consumed with things that quite often are not even there; and quite frankly even if they are there, so what?

So what if someone doesn't like you. There are over 7 billion people on this planet, they are not all going to like you are they? A tougher skin may be needed, because not everyone at work will be honest, kind or value you for who you are and what you can do. That is not your problem, that is theirs.

It is by no accident that our social media streams are awash with motivational messages and reminders about how many times J.K Rowling failed before she had a bestselling book on her hands. Or how many prototypes Dyson made before he had one that worked. It's because success has failure and winning at work has tough times. What if J.K Rowling had listened to publisher number three and given up and 'Got a real job' or if Dyson had stopped 'wasting his money on his inventions'.

"Success has failure and winning at work has tough times. "

Therefore, to get results you need to accept that not all people will like you, and that their thoughts are just that, theirs, and not the property of you. When you can do this, you can stay on track. One client was able to remember this and speak to competitors about what they did. Instead of making the assumptions that they would be thinking, 'You are here to steal our clients and ideas', they actually loved the idea that they could work together and take a 'bigger slice of the cake' and it lead to five more similar contracts that they could never have considered had they kept on assuming that everyone was thinking they were going to steal their business.

Can you see how dangerous worrying about what others are thinking can be for your career? If you worry you've not created a strong enough plan of action here, it may be a good idea to:

▶ Go back and create a more powerful negative circle. To really feel the pain that you are causing in your own success.

▶ Check that your goal is strong enough. Does it really ensure you stay focused on the prize you want?

▶ Remember the bubble game – sorry but you just aren't that interesting. What are people really thinking about?

▶ Write it, Rant it, Bin it. Play this game to see if you can really move forward. If not, do you have to face a conversation? Or is it enough to be able to accept that you are wasting your precious brain space on something that is detrimental to your success?

▶ Who can you rely on to keep you positively motivated? Who drags you down on social media? Just the wrong style of posts can stir your brain straight back to the worries of what everyone else is thinking. So be mindful of your choice of online friends. Are they keeping you motivated and inspired or damaging your success and mindset?

If you take these actions and remember the results that my clients have seen, you too could see that you could increase your chances of winning at work just by choosing to dump the cacophony of unhelpful thoughts loitering around in your head. Now that is scary and powerful, right?

11

I'm scared to ask for what I want

When I work with people who want to achieve big in their professional lives, it's amazing how many assumptions are made when it comes to asking for what you want. Highly intelligent, self-motivated, dedicated people let this fear impact on their success.

In the previous chapter we touched upon the damage that assumptions can make; however, in this chapter I really want to go to town on assumptions because I've seen the damage they cause. And I want to bring it to the table for everyone and deal with it for good. Let's make it public enemy number one for success and kick its butt into history!

 # F – Fear

Have you ever found yourself in front of an opportunity and thinking, 'I'm just not sure it's appropriate to ask this right now', or questioning, 'I don't know if this is something that they would be interested in', or 'You can't just go in and ask them can you'?

However, as I have learnt with so many clients over the years (and in my own career), in dealing with the fear of asking for what you want, you can really rocket your success. Conversely this chapter couldn't feature earlier in the book because you had to look at other areas of your own personal and professional development to be able to land at this chapter and be open minded enough to say, 'Yes Mand, I get this'.

When this fear is allowed to really dig its heels into your success it can manifest itself in so many ways. Yes, you can end up making dangerous assumptions that cost you opportunities, pay rises, promotions and accomplishments, but more than that it can:

▶ cause you to squander your precious time in tasks that don't actually deliver results (because you don't dare to do the things that could work);

▶ mean you never reach your full potential – ever;

▶ damage what you think of yourself and allow others to keep your success profile lowered. You in effect raise other people's profiles and diminish your own because you are too scared to ask for what you want.

The full horror of how big this fear can get and the impact it can have on your success can literally stop you in your tracks. The good news is that, like other fears in this book, it is one that doesn't take lots of skills to fix. It starts with what you choose to think. (Notice I say 'choose to think'.) As harsh as that may feel to say that to you, it is true that we choose to think what we think, and hopefully at this stage in this book you are understanding the power you could have over what you think.

We can't always control what gets delivered into our professional lives; however, we can have *control* over how we react to it. And when we don't ask for what we want, we are choosing to be reactive to something before we know what the action will be. It turns business into a science experiment!

66 ***We can't always control what gets delivered into our professional lives; however, we can have*** control *over how we react to it.* *99*

The problem is you may think that you ask for what you want; so do you *get* what you want?

If you don't, then I would suggest you are still fearful of asking for what you want, because you haven't mastered the skill of asking for what you want and getting it.

I've heard many people say, 'But I asked them and they said no' and when I've explored the details with them I've discovered in actual fact they've handled the situation in the wrong way. Yes, they may have asked for what they want, but in the wrong way; it could have been bad timing and they made the mistake of not asking again at a more opportune time (poor follow up is a costly mistake in your professional life and I've seen it impact on many!).

Using the wrong style of communication, the wrong timing, asking the wrong questions, speaking to the wrong person, presenting in the wrong way can all lead to a big 'No'. So if you feel you don't have the fear of asking for what you want, can you say you *get* what you want? If not let's work on that shall we?

66 ***Using the wrong style of communication, the wrong timing, asking the wrong questions, speaking to the wrong person, presenting in the wrong way can all lead to a big 'No'.*** *99*

E – Examples and exercises

Examples

This business owner had their business to grow. That had fallen into this business because of an enforced redundancy that had created a small business. However, they had a natural skill for hiding out in an office, talking to people on the phone. The products were good and the wholesaler was guaranteeing them the products for as long as they wanted them.

With the massive growth of the consumers' love of online sales, their company was finding it tough. Their online presence was poor; they didn't like or understand online marketing, and felt it wasn't right for their consumers or their products and services. There had to be another way.

Working with this business owner we talked about new ventures and worked out how to achieve them. As we worked together over the course of a morning we created a strategy and structure and basically came up with the 'Homework' that they would put into action to take the business forward to explore these new ventures. With any client you always look to check that the client has a clearly defined understanding of how it will fit in with their day-to-day schedule and so we physically pulled up their diary and started to work out where the work would fit in. This person then stopped and looked at me and said, 'But why would they want me? I can't go and ask for that!'

❝You can't dictate when someone buys; however, you can have a say in whom they buy from.❞

'I'm not an expert in what we've discussed, I just sell these products!' In this example I was working with a client to raise the company's profile, and to do that you have to appreciate that even the small company has to work out who their audience is and speak loudly and proudly to them. And to do *that* you have to be the expert for those people in your industry, showcasing the latest trends, ideas and guiding people, so that they understand everything they want to. As I like to say: 'You can't dictate when someone buys; however, you can have a say in whom they buy from,' and for this business owner this is what we were doing: raising their profile so that they could find their online voice for discerning customers who wanted quality. But still the issue was two-fold. 1) They held a limiting belief that said that someone else was the expert. This one always impresses me. That we hand the success to someone else because we have set the bar on our success lower. You will love the exercise to fix that! (2) The assumption that the solutions that we had come up with were not going to be wanted by the person I had suggested they contact.

When this fearful business owner (and yes we did run through the conversation using the skills and tools from Chapter 8) contacted the press and said, 'I think it could be great if I wrote for you every month to bring this subject to your audience', the editor didn't say no – they loved the idea. So much so, that within the year they were writing for three publications off of the back of that one, AND promoting many other businesses in the area, and were receiving a lot of attention for their company.

Within two years the business was well known in the area to the point that they were able to be involved with the top events in the area and be able to be given products from some of the best people in the industry to create competitions to further raise the company's profile. This business owner's company is now talked about in international circles by the crème de le crème of the industry. They have definitely raised their profile. And yet if they had not asked for what they wanted, the ball could never have started rolling. Scary, right?

NB. The fear was two-fold: (1) that they were not capable of being the expert of choice, and so many of us do that; (2) that the person that they would love to work with would not be interested.

Exercises

These exercises will help you change this fear and ask for what you want. But watch out world: it won't just happen in the work place! If you wanted to change the shape of your body, you wouldn't do just one exercise and expect to look that amazing at the end of the first day would you? So I'm sorry, but this chapter has three exercises. Don't groan. They aren't scary and huge. They are as big or as small as you choose to make them. See how I pass that back to you?

Exercise 1 – Stop giving your success to someone else

Don't worry if you have been doing this; I've been guilty of this in the past too. Nice people tend to do this. You are so intent on trying to make it a better world, you forget that some people are so intent on their own agenda that they really will do anything to get past you and so when you literally give them your opportunities, they won't slow down to take them.

If you are lucky you may get a thank you, but you won't get taken along for the success. So this is how to fix that.

▶ Before you big up someone else, *big up you*. Remember from Chapter 4 that you are not arrogant; this is not a full-blown 'Look at me world' strut around the work place thing – this is a quiet inner confidence that says 'I'm just as capable as that person is and here is why'. Big yourself up in your head. If you don't, why would anyone else? Then when it comes up in conversation, meetings or discussions you are able to confidently say something along the lines of, 'I feel that I could work well with Sam on this. We both have the skills for this; it could be a great opportunity for both of us'. I have an attitude that says that 'Success is better shared'. Bob Berg (one of the world's leading experts on this subject and an exceptional speaker and author) also speaks about creating win–win relationships. I first read his books many years ago and they resonated with me, because I realised that all good relationships in my career were like this and from then on I worked to create them in my life. The idea is that both parties walk away thinking that they have got a good deal: what they have wanted. And if you big up yourself *and* the other party, that is a win–win situation.

▶ Before you give it away, ask yourself this: '*Could I do this?*' I don't know if Richard Branson actually said this (you know that everything written on Facebook isn't actually true, right?), but I read that Branson said, 'Say "Yes", then work out how you will do it'. Whether he said it or not, that has been my approach long before I read that quote. In fact that is how I ended up speaking for international author and millionaire Mark Rhodes because when he asked 'Will you be a speaker on why coaching works at one of my success days' I said 'Yes' even though I was petrified of public speaking, didn't know how I was going to do it, what was involved or what was expected of me. So could you say 'Yes' and learn along the way? When you were little you didn't know what to do on the first day of school did you? When you had your first day at work you didn't know what was expected of you did you? You had to fight that fear, and it was only by taking action that you were able to learn and achieve.

▶ Replicate and educate: When you next go to give your success to someone else, ask yourself '*Why not me?* Although we've learnt in this book that the work place can be a tough environment with some people quite happy to tread over you to get to the top, not everyone is like that. As I've already shared, lots of people are very supportive and happy to mentor and coach you to succeed. In fact, recently I found myself in a situation where I was second guessing what I wanted to ask for, so in a private Facebook group (see Facebook can be proactive and supportive if used in the right way) I asked if it was taking the right action. In essence I wanted to be educated. And wise entrepreneurs gave me advice on what they would do and actually set my mind at rest that I had in actual fact asked for the right thing. So who can you ask for advice from? Who and what can you replicate? If you were prepared to give your success to someone else, what did you think that person had that you didn't? Study that and work out how you could replicate those skills. Acting the part is well on the road to being it. Yes, there is the possibility that you will need to learn new skills; however, you've got to know what you want to be like to achieve it.

Exercise 2 – What's stopping you?

With our example above I could see this business owner had real talent. I tend to see a client's full potential, long before they do! When I suggested they raise their profile and get themselves known as a thought leader it pushed them so far out of their comfort zone that they couldn't see it any more. This exercise was so powerful that it has stuck with them to this day, and it encourages them to take action when they find they are fighting a fear or procrastinating. I asked them, 'What's stopping you?' This stopped them in their tracks. 'What do you mean what's stopping me?' 'Well do you have something more pressing that needs dealing with today or this week? I thought you wanted to grow this business?' Calling someone's bluff on what they say they want to achieve after two hours of work is disgruntling at least and soul destroying at worse. You could see them asking themselves 'Am I really settling for this? Is this really what I'm prepared to accept as success?' Every time you are in a situation where it looks like you are going to give your success to someone else, ask yourself 'What is stopping me?'

Exercise 3 – Assumptions

"When you assume, you make an ass out of you and me."

I promised in this book that I would work on the assumptions that attack your success, because in my career as a coach I would say that I see assumptions cropping up, damaging people's success in most client sessions. Oscar Wilde summed it up when he said, 'When you assume, you make an ass out of you and me', and he was right. What are assumptions costing you?

▶ Do you assume that the person that didn't answer your email wasn't interested?

► Do you assume that because you are a small business or a sole trader that a larger business doesn't want to do business with you (there's plenty of evidence to the contrary!)

► Do you assume that 'Little people' like you don't hit the big time? Why not? Someone's got to!

► Do you assume you can't ask for promotion you've only been here five minutes!

All of these assumptions, and more, cost you success. They enable the fear of asking for what you want to stay strong and in power. You enable fear to stay, and you permit success to stay away. You need to learn to challenge your inner assumptions, and since you may not have a coach handy by your side. How can you do that?

Well with the first two exercises you can ensure you are not handing the opportunities away and challenging your thinking about your ability to succeed; however, what about when things do land on your doorstep? What if they are subtle and don't have a sign across their chests saying, 'Hello I'm a great opportunity that will rocket success and make your wildest dreams come true'. How do you ensure you don't miss those opportunities because you are assuming that you can't ask for what you want? What do you say to yourself then to ensure you don't assume the wrong thing, take the wrong actions and are too scared to ask for what you want?

Challenge your thoughts. In this chapter you will remember more than anything that it was about questions. In the Actions part of this chapter it will be about the art of asking the right questions of those around you. Now it's about tackling the damaging assumptions that stop you from asking for what you want. Really every thought, on everything you do for your career. ('That's a lot of thoughts Mandie!' I hear you cry. Don't worry, this is not forever; this is just to get you into a new habit of being aware of the way you *were* thinking and the new more powerful way of thinking that enables you to ask for what you want.)

If a job lands on your desk, what results do you want from this? Do you want to be remembered as someone who can rise to any challenge or as the office dogsbody? If it's the first, then ask for that. Tell people, the right people. In the right way. Think big, it's not just about this project, it's about your career. What do you want your boss to know you for? Have you told them that? People can't help you achieve if they don't know what it is you wish to achieve, can they? Likewise, if you are a networker, and regardless of if you work for someone else or run your own business it's a great way to stay connected, gain new business, get repeat business, learn new skills, stay in the loop and on people's radar. So it's something not to dismiss – as long as it's the right kind of networking for your industry. When networking, are you asking for what you want? It is not about shouting 'show me the money!' 'Give me the sale!' 'Buy me, Buy me, Buy me!' However, it is perfectly acceptable to say 'I'm looking to connect with HR Consultants' or 'I've been working with sales teams on their communication skills, and would love to talk to more companies looking to increase their success rate'. See, not salesy; however, you are asking for what you want. No assumptions, no sales, just politely asking for what you want. What would you ask for? And of whom?

Remember that by having clearly defined really focused goals you are far more likely to achieve them. Take assumptions out of your winning at work equation, and dramatically reduce your fear factors.

❝By having clearly defined really focused
goals you are far more likely to achieve them.❞

A – Actions

When you put together the power of the exercises and the action of this chapter is it not exciting that you could be asking for what you want and getting more of it? I think so. One of the issues you could be facing could be one that came up with a client who said. 'But I do ask for what I want, and I still don't get it!' When we looked at the details of their actions, we were able to see that their actions were always the same few. And if you are only doing the same few actions, then you have to know that you are getting them right, don't you?

And this person obviously wasn't. This is the power of asking the right question.

If we assume (ooh, dangerous word!) that you know what you want and are really focused on the right thing, then it's about ensuring you ask the right questions, and to do that you need to apply similar laws that you would as if they were someone you were looking to turn into a client (maybe you are looking to turn them into a client, in which case we are creating a short cut for you here!).

The big mistake people make when asking for what they want is they think about it from their view point and not the view point of the person they are asking. Turn the tables and imagine you are the person you want to say 'Yes' or to do what you want them to do:

- What matters to them?
- What do they need?
- Why should they say 'Yes'?
- What is in it for them?

Know their needs, wants, desires and stresses. Before you even ask for what you want, research these things for the other party. However, don't then plan to spend the next five minutes cramming all of what you know into a conversation. Just because you know it, it doesn't mean that person needs a reminder on their life story!

Good questioning means you:

- Ask the right questions at the right times. Achieve this by asking 'Is this the right time to speak?'
- Be respectful. If they say 'No', don't launch into what you wanted to talk about anyway, be it in the hallway at work or leaving an event or on the phone: if they said they were dashing, let them. Prepare an answer that respects that, for instance, 'No worries, I will email you to arrange a phone chat, within 24 hours.' (Be time specific; it shows intent, professionalism, and that you will do what you say you will.)
- Don't over talk. That means listening. Create space for them to talk. You are prepared, which means you can add to the conversation to back up what they are saying by using your researched information. (Remember you want to know why you are calling and you want to get that result; however, you do not want to ram that down their throat from the start of the call.) Win–win conversations create relationships; people like to support the success of people that are respectful of them.

 # R – Result

When I think of the results of fixing this fear it makes me smile. So many times, I've challenged a person's belief about asking for what they want, and they've gone on to do the strategies and ideas in this chapter with exceptional results. This fear has been destroyed and ultimate dreams and professional goals have been achieved:

- Like the business mum who told the company that she was working for on a part-time contract basis that she wanted to work fewer hours and to charge them more because she was going to set up her own business. She did it and in less than two years went from a kitchen-table business to employing two staff and not needing the contract work at all, just because she overcame the fear of asking for what she wanted.

▶ Like the person who passionately dreamed of being on the stage instead of in the audience yet was too afraid to ask how that could happen. (Okay they did have to work with me and use the contents of Chapter 7 too.) Now they speak on the national circuit for business owners in their area of expertise.

"Fear has a habit of sneaking in and creeping into our subconscious and hiding out there and we can be completely unaware until it is too late."

There is no doubt that this is a fear that is big and there is no doubt that unless you use Exercise 3 once in a while to check that you are still challenging your thoughts, you could slip back into bad habits. So please do promise me that you will be aware of these exercises and maybe revisit them once a year if you are feeling confident, just to ensure you stay that confident: fear has a habit of sneaking in and creeping into our subconscious and hiding out there and we can be completely unaware until it is too late. When I worked in the car industry we told our customers to get straight back into a car after an accident, because the longer you left it the more likely you were not to get back into a car for a while and possibly create a fear or nervousness of driving. Fear likes to take hold and if you don't monitor your results, your beliefs and your fear levels it could be loitering in the depths of your mind and sniping away at your success.

"Fear loves a flabby brain!"

Remember your brain is a giant muscle and as one fabulous business woman and PE instructor shouted out across the room at a BWN event recently when I asked what happens to muscles if we don't look after them: 'They get flabby!' Don't let that happen to your brain. Fear loves a flabby brain!

12

I can't take time out

F – Fear

I was once in a very important meeting that I and another member of the board had spent a lot of time prepping for and as we shook hands on the work, my business friend and colleague said, 'you can call us 24 hours a day, 7 days a week'. I smiled and shook the gentleman's hand and said, 'I promise we will work incredibly hard for you and deliver above and beyond what we say; however, I won't be answering my phone at 10 pm on a Sunday night, that is my family's time.' As we established in Chapter 1, my family is a value to me that I will rarely sacrifice. And it would have to be pretty dire for me to need to be on the phone at one in the morning wouldn't it? I was being honest and credible, although my business colleague gave me a sly dirty look that basically screamed 'what are you doing!'

What I was doing was laying down some ground rules. I would do anything for my clients. I would go well beyond the call of duty. However, am I going to be the person you call at two in the morning? Highly unlikely. Is it fearful to say that when there is a big contract on the line? It was definitely for my business partner; however, the gentleman whose hand I shook looked at me with a serious look (that did make me panic for a milli-second) and then he laughed and said, 'You are right, what could I possibly need to ring you about at two in the morning that couldn't wait until eight when it comes to marketing. We are too demanding of each other aren't' we.'

> **❝This fear that you can't take time out, that your success will collapse if you do or that someone else will swoop in and steal your success is madness.❞**

And yet I have sat with so many clients that will tell me that the tablet or laptop is going on their 25th Anniversary cruise. Or that they couldn't possibly turn their phone off for two weeks' holiday, 'How could they cope without me!', or that they will just 'do a little bit of planning over the weekend, it's not really work is it?' This non-stop brain activity may seem conscientious, and be leading to your big professional goals; however, this fear that you can't take time out, that your success will collapse if you do or that someone else will swoop in and steal your success is madness. However, it's madness that can manifest in ways far worse than just feeling guilt that you let your family members down (again) or overloaded your work colleagues. It can lead to:

▶ illness
▶ sleepless nights

- exhaustion
- divorce
- estranged children
- violence
- medication abuse
- mental health illness
- accidents
- poor work performance
- costly mistakes

And a lot more.

Do you think I'm laying this one on too thick? I remember years ago I was in the South of France with my father walking down a gravel lane surrounded by Eucalyptus trees, Mimosa and Cork tress and we were on a campsite predominately with static caravans owned by business owners and professionals. The caravans ranged in value from £25k to £100k. I can remember as a child listening to Dad speak to a gentleman that owned a number of department stores across the UK who was saying of all the holidays he had in the world, his favourite were his summers in a pair of shorts poking a barbie of lobsters with a glass of local chateau wine in hand. A few years later as Dad and I walked down one of the scented lanes we laughed at how sad the talk was:

'They aren't coming this year; he's had a heart attack.'

'They've had to give up travelling; she's got skin cancer.'

The list went on and on. And it helped us to quickly get over our fear of taking time out of our professional lives and our focused drive for success, because it was such a visual example. I can still clearly see my father turning to me with the sound of the cicadas in the background and saying, 'I don't want to be the richest man in the graveyard'.

"As much as success needs vision, self-belief, goals, focus and action sometimes it also needs you to have the confidence to take time out."

As much as success needs vision, self-belief, goals, focus and action sometimes it also needs you to have the confidence to take time out. It doesn't need to be a summer in the South of France; however, you do need to learn to listen to your body. Winning at work does actually need a body to do that in.

E – Examples and exercises

Example

The person was driven and dedicated. If their career needed more knowledge they didn't just research it, they gained a degree: that was how dedicated they were.

This meant that this person had so many skills that whenever a new opportunity came up it was hard to work out what the best course of action was. So they tended to throw themselves into it, not really pausing to work out if it was the right course of action. Just going for it, because it presented itself. This put a massive pressure on them, especially when a family member suddenly needed their help too. It was too much and they felt overwhelmed. It was impacting on their work; however, it was ridiculous to suggest they could do less. They'd just taken on more and now they had a member of their family to look after; it was impossible to see a way through.

We looked at this person's attitude to life, work, their beliefs, values. Where they liked to holiday (they couldn't see how that was of relevance either) and it became apparent that this person had been instilled with a very strong work ethic from a very young age. Their father had owned their own business and because their mother had been poorly he had run the home and made a successful business so that they and their siblings wanted for nothing. As we discussed this further they realised he had a habit as he was cleaning the house and they had said they were feeling sick when it was bed time of saying things like, 'I clean this house, look after you kids and run a business, you don't hear me moan about being poorly do you?' This person had grown up being told that you don't take time off work, you work through, you battle through, if you want anything in life you have got to fight for it. We worked on the belief they held and broke each one down and gave this person a new more powerful way of thinking, a way of thinking that would enable them to create a more powerful way of working too. For instance, 'You have to fight for it; is it healthy to be fighting? Is fight a positive emotion or a negative one? Would you like to fight for what you want in life or would you like to easily achieve it?

The new way of thinking led to more respect for their body. They didn't work until they dropped. They learnt to outsource and share the load. They also realised that they weren't the only person on the planet that was capable of doing these things. By dropping the reins for a second, someone else invariably didn't pick them up, and if they didn't this person was gaining a new respect from others because they always had the reins! How did they do that?

Instead of being someone that did everything, this person did what they wanted to do for their success and what was respectful to themselves too. Yes, there were times when that was not possible, especially with their family member; however, at work it led to them being noticed more, because they didn't fight everyone else's fires so often and were more focused on what mattered to them. Having the confidence to say this and to take time out from work changed their lives in many ways. Not just at work.

"Instead of being someone that did everything, this person did what they wanted to do for their success and what was respectful to themselves too."

Exercise 1 – Rocketing your BCR

One of the reasons we are so scared to take time out is because we fear what is going on while our backs our turned:

▶ I bet so and so has completely wrecked that project and I will have to redo it all on Monday!

▶ They don't listen to me; it's going to cause a mountain of work for me. I should never have left the office.

▶ If I'm not there I know so and so will take the praise for this work and get my promotion too. He/she'd stab me in the back the second my back was turned!

▶ If I'm not there I bet something really cool will happen and I will miss out! Typical!

▶ If I go out they will only do it wrong.

▶ If I'm not here, they will just talk about me and make me look bad!

▶ I can't take time off, I don't earn any money if I'm not here.

▶ I can't take time off, this business doesn't run itself!

If any of these resonate with you then you need to rocket your BCR: your branding, your credibility and your reputation. Even if you work for someone else's business, you as a person looking to win at work need to be the equivalent of the brand that everyone wants to own. Before you walk in the room your name should be synonymous with what you do. If it is, you can be anywhere in the world and still win at work. Don't believe me? Sneak a peek at the results segment of this chapter. It's one of the things I love helping people to achieve: to get themselves and their businesses known and loved. How cool would it be that before you say a word, someone walks up to you and says, 'I've just been told that you are the expert for X and I need to speak to you'. Wouldn't it be great if people came to you, instead of the other way around? Wouldn't it be great if you came back from that break that recharged your brain and body and boosted your creativity to find that new opportunities had landed in your inbox and you'd done nothing!

So how can you build your BCR?

Branding, credibility and reputation are interlinked. It's about building a quality of service and standard around everything you do, and say and ensuring you deliver on that and protect it.

1 **Build your brand** – think about how you represent yourself, wherever you go or are: online and offline, and not just professional accounts. If I look you up on Facebook will I see someone falling out of a taxi rather drunk at three in the morning? Is that the professional brand you want to be synonymous with? Think about the big professional goals you have and what matters to people in those industries. Wherever you are, you need to represent that. Be your own brand.

2 **Cultivate your credibility** – you do this by phoning someone back at exactly the time you say you will. Emailing what and when you said you would. Delivering projects when you promised them. Remember the words synonymous with your industry? How do you get yourself known as an expert in this arena? Become a trusted standard and a person that can be relied on. Even if it is something un-work related, deliver on it.

3 **Rocket your reputation** – You do this by developing the first two first. You can't have a reputation until you prove yourself. However, when you do create the first two, use the third to protect all three.

You will become someone that is respected by knowing what you stand for and why you stand for them and going out of your way to prove that these are the things that matter to you, and you are prepared to stick your brand, credibility and reputation on them. People want to work with people they can rely on who they know will deliver. Knowing you do the right things by those around you and by yourself, could give you the strength to say, 'I have faith in my professional success and I can take time out'.

If you need more, let's look at another reason why we are scared to step away and take time out. Think about it logically: if you send out a clear message that you are available 24 hours a day, 7 days a week, what does that say about you?

Being a one-trick pony may seem good to you, however, more and more 21st-century business is realising that success, productivity, creativity and profitability comes down to more than just making your staff work hard and paying them well. Research is pointing to the fact that, despite the latest technologies that should be revolutionising the way we work, we are actually no more productive than we were in the 1960s. And worse still because we insist on being chained to our desks and online 24/7 we are losing out on success, productivity, creativity and profitability.

And I personally see this with clients who are so scared of stepping away from work for a little while. If you want success you will need to showcase to yourself and those around you that you are capable of doing other things. The gentleman who thought he was impressive because he 'doesn't do lunch' and ends up carrying his holiday forward to next year is not that impressive when you know that the clever winning companies are actively encouraging the staff to go and do something else for a little while to recharge the brain and come up with the solutions that seem to remain elusive. So this exercise will help you work on it. Because knowing something is the right thing to do and doing it is not the same thing is it?

Exercise 2 – 1, 2, 3

The next time you justify working late, taking the phone to the restaurant, powering up your laptop by the pool or postponing a holiday, reason with yourself 1, 2, 3. Does this fit into the three things that matter most to you in your life? Remember the core values exercise from Chapter 1?

What are your core values? Number 1? Number 2? and Number 3? Can you reason with yourself that your action is taking you towards those values?

"Be aware of your inner politician, who can deviate, deflect and skirt around any subject."

Think about your goals from Chapter 2. Can you reason that this action genuinely fits with those?

If you can hand on heart say it does, then go for it. However, be aware of your inner politician, who can deviate, deflect and skirt around any subject; who can massage your ego and mind into believing the wrong actions are the right ones. For instance:

'I reason it is perfectly acceptable to take my laptop on our wedding anniversary weekend away because the office is working on this big contract and although I've done my parts and I trust the team to get it right, if they have concerns I want them to know I'm a conscientious person who cares about them, the results and the company's future. And this fits into my values of family time, success and wealth because I'm honouring all three.'

Perfect politician reasoning. So let's reframe this shall we?

By taking your laptop on holiday what message are you sending to your partner? 'Yes darling I do love you, it's just I can't give you my undivided attention for 48 hours because my work success is more important than my relationship success with you.'

By telling the 'team' you are available you are saying that you don't trust them and the only person that could possibly get it right is you, because you are the best and let's be honest far better than any of them. 'So I know you will need me and actually I've little faith in you. I don't even trust you to look after something over a weekend when the office is predominantly shut for 48 hours.'

How do these reframed statements feel?

As with all things, we have the power to frame things in the light we choose to. Think about something that hangs on a wall in your office or home or somewhere you go. Imagine picking it up and putting it somewhere else, would it work anywhere and everywhere you put it? It's doubtful and it's the same with your thinking. Don't let your brain psyche you into thinking you are right to never take time out.

Reframe your responses and apply 1, 2, 3. The most important things in your world to you, your values and goals. Are they really being respected and honoured?

You may be able to maintain the constant of never taking time out; however, for how long? And at what cost? And is it a cost you are really prepared to accept?

And is it really creating the success and the wins you want it to?

A – Actions

Only you know

Remember only you will know what actions you are taking. Only you will know what your goals are, unless you are telling everyone; so, how can anyone steal your success? While you are away from your work, how will anyone know what your objectives are and what you are aiming for? Thus you can take time out safe in the knowledge that your plans to win at work are safely locked up in your mind, and you are creating the space for your brain to work on them.

"Only you will know what your goals are unless you are telling everyone; so, how can anyone steal your success?"

You wouldn't try and run marathons back to back. Why? Because it's not good for you. So why do you assume it's good to work day after day with no brain space?

Driven and dedicated are the ones most likely to suffer from the fear of not being able to take time out therefore reframe it. You are not taking time out, you are taking a different action to power up your creativity, productivity and success.

Outsource, delegate and automate

To take time out to win at work you need to learn these skills.

Outsourcing means that you have literally less to do, so that you can do the things that matter more to your success. It is scary the first time you give your work to someone else to do, and yes they may not do it the exact same way as you; however, you could learn some new ways of working and top tips from them too. Importantly, if someone is doing the mundane, non-money making, not aiming for success tasks, it means you can be doing the money-making aiming for success task.

Delegating not only does you good, it turns you into an enabler. Instead of being someone selfish who takes all the chances for success, self-development and chances to shine for yourself, by delegating you are sharing them around. And by delegating you are freeing up your time.

Automation is a brilliant tool. You can automate your marketing: emails, banking, research. Do a little research for yourself to find what could work for you and the basic rule is if it's something you do a lot of and don't need to really think about doing then there's a good chance it can be automated in some way. This will enable you to look ultra-efficient too.

Action – Have you tried mind mapping?

Tony Buzan was the inventor of this fabulous tool for organising your thoughts, ideas and success, and it's one I use to plan speaking engagements, training courses, even this book. Instead of seeing taking time out as something to be avoided at all cost, how do you feel about creating the space to take your success to the next level by grabbing a pad and some coloured pens and exploring what your creative mind is trying to tell you? Not at your desk. Not on a laptop, tablet or phone. Old-fashioned: get your creative juices flowing, pen and paper.

Your first exploration into thinking could be: 'Things I would do if I was wasn't working'. Remember to add everything and don't let time, money, skill or commitments restrict your ideas. Just allow the ideas to pour onto the paper. Remember, the more you write, the deeper you are exploring and the more likely you are to find something that will enable your brain to properly switch off from work mode for a little while and really power up your ability to win at work.

After you've explored that, instead of dashing straight back to work why not take action. Ironically the action could be to sit and listen to the bird song, do some gardening, paint, get on your bike/horse/feet! What hobbies do you love but have neglected? I often see that successful highly focused people have dropped their hobby time and switched it for more work and actions they think will get them to their big professional goals. However, as with most things in life it needs balance, and when they've brought the horse riding, the acting, the singing or the motor bike back into their days, suddenly they are getting better results. One person said, 'I feel like I'm me again, I've never felt more alive!' What does that do for your mindset and your ability to stay focused and positive?

Still considered one of the greatest mathematical minds in history, Archimedes famously shouted 'Eureka' as he stepped into the bath. He had one of his moments of greatness not with quill in hand poised ready to write something brilliant to annoy the hell out of 21st-century children, but when having a wash! What actions do you intend to take to power up your success? How will you ensure you can create the space to have Eureka moments that could literally help you win at work?

 # R – Results

Ask yourself who would you rather do business with: people that are happy and loving life or those that look on the edge of a nervous breakdown?

I think we have an amazing opportunity here thanks to the 21st-century communications explosion to be part of a revolution that enables every person to be the person that they want to be. Living a life that fulfils them and enables them to succeed, that does not entail four hours' commute, 90+ hour weeks, no loved-one time or social lives, or embarrassment when you tell people you have kids. But it does mean you have to take a stand and say things like 'really sorry, I'm finishing work now'.

If you want results you've got to power up your reasons why so that you can read this and imagine real pain, if you don't deal with the fear of taking time out. One business owner who told me they sent emails at all times of the day and night and their clients loved that they would get a report at 3 am ready for the next working day found this fear laughable. 'I'm making lots of money; I've got a dream house, this works.' It didn't keep working. They found themselves in hospital on a drip a mere few months later.

> **"If you want results you've got to power up your reasons why so that you can read this and imagine real pain, if you don't deal with the fear of taking time out."**

Another successful person realised that they were in actual fact a terrible role model for their children. If they worked all day and all night, were they saying that was what they wanted for their children? Did they want their children to not see their children? Did they want their children to miss out on teaching their children to ride a bike or read a book? It was the right level of pain that enabled them to bring balance back into their life. Ironically it was the action of doing hobbies with the children that gave them the brain space to work out what they needed to do next to take their success to the next level.

And for myself I had 42 days' holiday last year. My phone was so dead that I didn't know where it was! And yet I came back to new business and opportunities that were beyond what I could have hoped for and some free PR too! A big learning curve from the woman who did everything yesterday and answered everyone's email the same day, regardless of who or what they wanted. And I now attract clients that respect me completely when I say that we need to get booked in advance because I'm away at this time with my family. Because let's be honest I want to help everyone achieve win–win relationships and success and so the skills, tools and techniques I share with you in this book are the ones that bring the kind of clients that make work a joy and never feel like work.

You see not all success is achieved by being focused on the goal. Sometimes you do need to actually give your brain the space to work on it too. If you are constantly adding more and more information, questions and jobs to your head, how is it supposed to come up with the solutions and the ideas?

Thank you

Thank you for reading this book. I say this because I'm actually thanking your brain that is whirring away thinking of new ideas already. You may not appreciate that it is doing this; however, as I like to call them with clients, create back burners: ideas that you create and let simmer away in the corner of your mind. So thank you reader's brain, because I know long after you put this book down, you are going to be creating great ways to take you to the next stages of success.

So be kind to your brain. Give it rest, and fun, laughter and happiness. Feed it well and water it often. Be very aware that fear is a devious sneaky evil toad, that will do its very best to creep back into your professional life. It is only by revisiting these chapters and being aware of the things that you resist and don't tackle that you will be able to spot the fears hiding out in your mind and doing their best to reinstate their power over you.

But don't worry. Remember, with this book you have learnt and will go on to master transferable skills that can be used in so many areas of your life:

▶ the negative to positive spiral;

▶ the 'What if' game – good version and bad;

▶ the 'Why I'm awesome' two-page written A4 document;

▶ the values exercise – are you valuing and appreciating yours? – This may alter as your success increases so do revisit this to check you are still working and planning in alignment with your core values;

▶ pain and pleasure;

▶ your natural style;

▶ the power of No;

▶ the art of questions.

And so many others!

The last thing you need to do is ask yourself;

'What actions am I going to take, when and what impact is it going to have on my success?'

And if you don't;

'What are you agreeing to?'

What did you think of this book?

We're really keen to hear from you about this book, so that we can make our publishing even better.

Please log on to the following website and leave us your feedback.

It will only take a few minutes and your thoughts are invaluable to us.

www.pearsoned.co.uk/bookfeedback

Index

INDEX

focus 66, 118, 121, 126–7
  and goals 8, 23, 76, 121, 122, 123, 126, 137, 151
  ways to keep focused 121–2

gate keepers
  and phoning people 101–2
goals/goal setting 4, 16–25, 147
  action 23–4
  and assumptions 123
  breaking down of 21–3
  and comfort zone 23–4
  examples 18–19
  fear of 16–18
  focused 8, 23, 76, 121, 122, 123, 126, 137, 151
  need for clearly defined 11
  power goals 19–20, 120–3
  power of words 20–1
  privacy of 25
  questions to ask yourself 22–3
  result 24–5
  and teachers 16
  unachievable 24

hands
  and public speaking 85
hecklers
  dealing with during public speaking 88–9
help, asking for 54–64, 68
  actions 60–3
  automatic response 56
  common beliefs 54
  examples 55–6
  fear od 54–5
  identifying your natural style 62–3
  impact of not 61
  listing negatives and positives of 59–60
  negative spiral time 56–60
  results 63–4
  and success 57
hiding your real self 2–14
  action 8–9
  examples 3–4

impact on success 11
result 9–14
values exercise 4–8
hobbies 4, 150, 151

influencers
  and success 38–40
inner confidence 8, 12, 45, 50–1, 52, 88, 134

jargon
  and public speaking 88

listening 138
  and phoning people 103–4

McLean, Colin 86
mind mapping 149–50

natural style
  identifying and finding your 62–3, 73–4, 113
  and public speaking 86
  and saying no 73–5
negative spiral
  and asking for help 56–60
  and not believing you can succeed 31–4
  and public speaking 83
networks/networking 39, 90, 118, 136–7
Nike 40
no, saying 66–77
  actions 75–6
  and 'can you just-ers' 66, 68, 69–71
  Catherine Wheel effect 66–8
  example 68–9
  fear of 66–8
  and politicians 76
  power of words 72
  repercussions game 72–3
  results 76–7
  'what' questions 72
  and 'what if' game 72–3
  and your natural style 73–5
'no' word
  and phoning people 100–1

156